FROM MINISKIRT TO HIJAB

From
MINISKIRT
to HIJAB

A Girl in Revolutionary Iran

JACQUELINE SAPER

POTOMAC BOOKS
An imprint of the University of Nebraska Press

Library of Congress Cataloging-in-Publication Data
Names: Saper, Jacqueline, 1961– author.
Title: From miniskirt to hijab: a girl in
revolutionary Iran / Jacqueline Saper.
Description: [Lincoln]: Potomac Books, an
imprint of the University of Nebraska Press,
[2019] | Includes bibliographical references.
Identifiers: LCCN 2019001978
ISBN 9781640121171 (cloth: alk. paper)
ISBN 9781640122420 (epub)
ISBN 9781640122437 (mobi)
ISBN 9781640122444 (pdf)
Subjects: LCSH: Saper, Jacqueline,
1961—Childhood and youth. | Jewish
women—Iran—Biography. | Iran—History—
Revolution, 1979—Personal narratives, Jewish.
Classification: LCC DS135.1653 S27 2019 |
DDC 955.05/42092 [B]—dc23 LC record
available at https://lccn.loc.gov/2019001978

Set in Garamond Premier by E. Cuddy.
Designed by N. Putens.

In memory of my resilient father, Rahmat Lavi, who loved his native country of Iran, and to my courageous mother, Stella Averley, who loved my father enough to leave her native England.

And to all those whose lives have been interrupted by revolution and war.

بنی آدم اعضای یک پیکرند

که در آفرینش ز یک گوهرند

چو عضوی به درد آوَرَد روزگار

دگر عضوها را نمانَد قرار

تو کز محنت دیگران بی‌غمی

نشاید که نامت نهند آدمی

Human beings are like parts of a body,

created from one essence.

When one part is hurt and in pain,

others cannot remain in peace and quiet.

If the misery of others leaves you indifferent

    and with no feeling of sorrow,

then you cannot be called a human being.

*"Bani Adam" (The Children of Adam), by
thirteenth-century Persian poet Sa'adi Shirazi.*

*The lines of this poem are displayed on the
wall at the entrance to the United Nations
building in New York City. This poem,
using the translation above, was included in
President Carter's toast to the Shah of Iran
during the New Year's Eve 1978 State Dinner
at Niavaran Palace in Tehran.*

CONTENTS

ILLUSTRATIONS

ACKNOWLEDGMENTS

I would like to thank the many individuals who enthusiastically encouraged me to record this story. To my parents, Stella and Rahmat, who taught me to navigate life's challenges with strength and fortitude; to my husband, Ebi, my life partner, who is my best friend and my greatest supporter; and to my children who seized every opportunity our immigration to the United States afforded them and who are now accomplished adults in their own right. To my editor, Lisa Thaler, who asked the right questions and with her keen insights evoked details that I never would have included. Finally, to the professional staff at the University of Nebraska Press, for bringing my manuscript to life.

HISTORICAL NOTE

Once known as Persia, Iran is a modern nation with an ancient past. Two and a half thousand years ago, Cyrus the Great was crowned the first king of the Persian Empire. He is known to have respected the traditions and customs of the various subjects of his vast empire. The Persian monarchy continued throughout the centuries, and each dynasty had a unique history with distinctive characteristics.

In 1925, Reza Shah established the Pahlavi dynasty. He was a Western-leaning monarch who took drastic and unorthodox measures to modernize the country. For example, in 1936, the king banned the wearing of hijab for women and traditional Eastern garb for men.

His son Mohammad Reza Shah became king in 1941 and ruled Iran through an era of rapid modernization and prosperity until 1979. The Iranian Revolution of 1979 ended the establishment of the monarchy in Iran and replaced it with an Islamic republic.

The Shah left Iran on a cold winter day in January of 1979 on a flight to Egypt. While delivering one of his last speeches to his fellow countrymen, he uttered these words predicting the implications of his departure from his homeland: "If I leave, Iran will go down. If Iran goes down, the Middle East will go down. If the Middle East goes down, the world will suffer."[1]

FROM MINISKIRT TO HIJAB

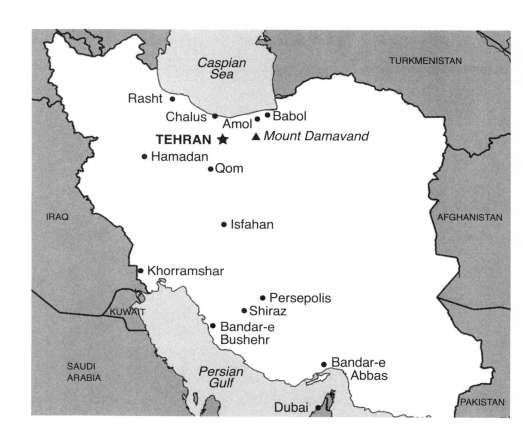

MAP OF IRAN.

PART 1

Hope

1961–1978

CHAPTER I

The Best of Both Worlds

My bicultural upbringing in the upper-middle-class northern Tehran community of Yousefabad was evident in our home's décor. Silk Persian carpets and traditional *khatam* handicraft inlaid-mosaic picture frames sat amid oil paintings of the English countryside and blue Wedgwood porcelain.

Both of my parents' cultures placed great emphasis on tea. A large, silver-toned samovar sat on the kitchen counter next to a china pot of fragrant English breakfast tea and was left simmering on a low setting for hours. My dad elevated the preparation of tea to an art form. Just as if he were in one of his chemistry labs at the university, he would carefully measure a spoonful of loose tea into the mesh infuser of the teapot. When the water was almost boiling, he would fill the ceramic teapot halfway, cover it, and let the tea (*chai*) steep for about five minutes on top of the samovar's lid. As is the Iranian custom, my father drank his chai from a glass (*estekan*) to better assess its quality and consistency of color. Our traditional Isfahan tea set included a hammered silver tray and six estekans. A three-legged, lidded bowl with a handle contained the lump sugar and thin, transparent yellow disks—Isfahani candies known as *poolaki*.

For Mom, the rules changed. Whereas Dad was precise, Mom was delicate. Dad would pour her tea into a fine English bone china cup with a saucer, leaving space at the top to add milk. Mom never drank her tea black and told me that the extra milk is "the English way, Jacqueline."

Mom and Dad loved to take their tea in the grand living room, seated on the navy-and-cream sofa, with the sun streaming in through the floor-to-ceiling panoramic windows. The windows overlooked the balcony and our private garden. Among the many fruit trees, including mulberry, sour cherry, and apple, Dad's favorite was the persimmon tree. Its graceful branches reached over and partly covered the pond; and from its prodigious harvest, we made gift baskets for our friends and neighbors. There were red, white, and yellow roses, and at the other end of the garden, in front of the watermelon bushes, lay a few rows of chrysanthemums and violets.

We also had a view of the snowcapped Alborz Mountains. In springtime, when the snow melted and after it rained, the *joobs* (water channels) on the side streets of Tehran filled with water that had traveled downstream from the slopes to the north. When we opened the windows, we could hear the melody of the trickling stream. My siblings, Raymond and Victoria, and I would throw pebbles into the channels and chase them as they flowed away.

The most prominent of the few religious artifacts in our home was a mezuzah affixed to the frame of our front door. The stunning transparent cylinder was decorated with gold crowns and the Hebrew letter *shin*, which is the first letter of the *Shema* prayer that is written on parchment and contained in the case. The prayer is an affirmation of the Jewish people's faith in God.

Every room in our four-bedroom house had tiled marble floors partly covered with colorful handwoven Persian rugs. Each was a work of art, with a center medallion and an intricate pattern or an overall curvilinear design of birds and flowers. Dad said that our Persian rugs were made in Isfahan and, thus, were "top tier." He would carefully remove his shoes before walking on them. His favorite was the blue-and-cream carpet in the living room that complemented the sofa. Beaming with pride, Dad would show off its "eighty knots per centimeter" to visitors, turning back a corner.

In the family room, a crystal chandelier hung from the tall ceiling, and a Seiko wall clock chimed on the hour. Raymond, Victoria, and I listened to records by Bob Dylan, Tom Jones, and Santana on the large oak music console. Nestled on the burgundy leather couches and matching ottoman, we would all watch the Schaub Lorenz television, our window to the world.

*

My parents met in September of 1947, at a social dance for University of Birmingham students. My father, Rahmat, was a foreign student in the chemical engineering department. He, along with five other students from the Petroleum University of Technology in the southern city of Abadan, Iran, had been awarded an all-expenses-paid scholarship to pursue their education in England. My mother, Stella, was pursuing a degree in journalism and also took shorthand courses.

At the end of the school term, my father returned to his homeland of Iran, and a long-distance courtship ensued. For two years, Rahmat and Stella exchanged love letters and photographs by post. I had read some of these letters, dating to the late 1940s. I found the intimate correspondence to be a testament to their love and commitment to each other. The fact that my parents had chosen each other added to the rarity of their courtship, because at that time, most marriages in Iran, for Jews and Muslims alike, were arranged. Finally, in May 1950, their engagement was announced in Birmingham's *Jewish Chronicle,* despite their physical separation and the long distance between them. The news of my father's engagement spread throughout the community, and soon after Stella received a letter of congratulation.

Tehran, Iran, 6th June, 1949

Miss Stella Averley,
239 Lichfield Rd.,
Aston Birmingham,
England

Dear Miss,

I am Ben. R. Mayeri, a native of Isfahan, and an old friend to Mr. R. Lavi.

I heard the good news of your engagement to Mr. Lavi through himself. I hope you will not think it out of place in me to write you this short note of congratulation on your good fortune.

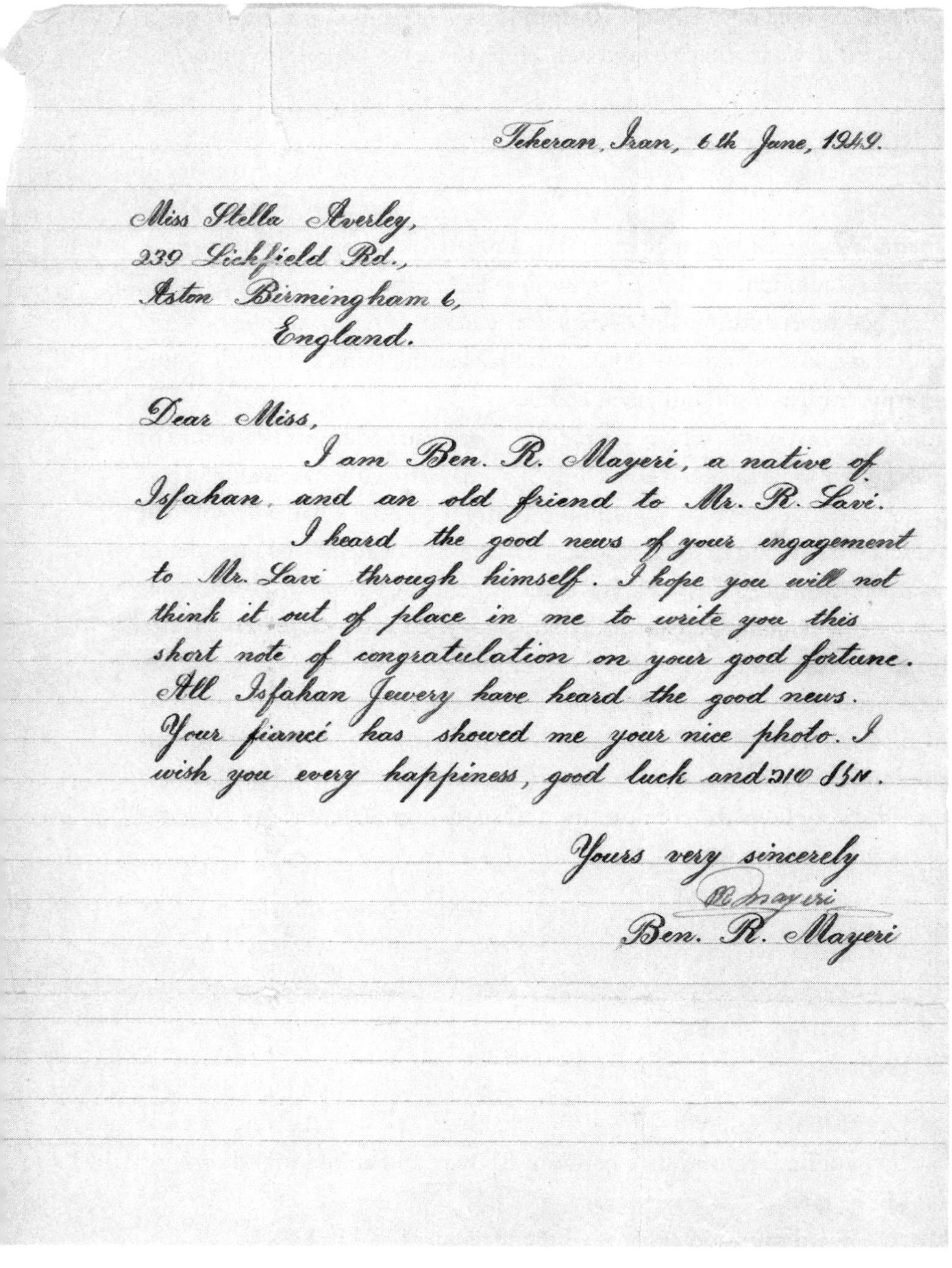

Teheran, Iran, 6th June, 1949.

Miss Stella Averley,
239 Lichfield Rd.,
Aston Birmingham 6,
England.

Dear Miss,

I am Ben. R. Mayeri, a native of Isfahan, and an old friend to Mr. R. Savi.

I heard the good news of your engagement to Mr. Savi through himself. I hope you will not think it out of place in me to write you this short note of congratulation on your good fortune. All Isfahan Jewery have heard the good news. Your fiancé has showed me your nice photo. I wish you every happiness, good luck and מזל טוב.

Yours very sincerely

Ben. R. Mayeri

FIG. 1. Congratulatory letter written and mailed to England by a member of the Isfahan Jewish community, on the occasion of my parents' engagement, 1949.

All Isfahan Jewry have heard the good news. Your fiancé has showed me your nice photo. I wish you every happiness and good luck and *Mazel tov* (congratulations, written in Hebrew).

Yours Very Sincerely,
Ben. R. Mayeri

My mother, Stella, made the difficult decision to leave her family and her native country of England and to resettle in Iran and marry Rahmat. In late December 1950, Stella boarded a plane at Heathrow Airport and flew to Tehran. At Mehrabad Airport, she was introduced to Rahmat's family. His parents, Jacob (Yaghoub) and Shoshana, showered Stella with kisses and welcomed her with an elegant gold bracelet and other gifts. Rahmat's older sister, Pouran, and her husband and children, along with his younger brother, Darius, were also present. Many more members of the community had also made the drive to the airport to witness the unusual phenomenon of the arrival of Rahmat's foreign fiancée.

Two days later, Rabbi Yedidia Shofet, the chief rabbi of Tehran's Jewish community, officiated at my parents' wedding ceremony. Since Stella didn't understand Farsi, Rabbi Shofet explained the service to her through a translator. During the ceremony, Stella was presented with a beautiful *naqdeh* (custom and handmade shawl), made from delicate sheer fabric in white, and embellished with gold-thread embroidery. The bride and groom, along with witnesses, signed the *ketubah* (Jewish marriage agreement) and then the *sanad-e ezdevaj* (the official Iranian marriage license). Rabbi Shofet praised the bride for her courage and her devotion. He blessed the unconventional couple, wishing them a long married life, filled with happiness and many children.

*

My brother, Raymond, who had the same initials as my dad, was born in 1952. My sister, Victoria, who was named after the British Queen Victoria, was born in 1956. Every year on October 26 we teased Victoria that the strings of twinkling red and green lights and flashing neon models of royal crowns that hung throughout the city were in her honor. That is because she shared a birthday with the sovereign, Mohammad Reza Shah Pahlavi.

FIG. 2. Me, age three, with my mother, Stella, in Tehran, 1964.

The Shah's birthday was a national holiday and was celebrated with enthu-siasm and jubilation.

One year my family lined up on the side of Pahlavi Avenue just north of Crown Prince Square and joined the crowds of people who patiently waited for the arrival of the royal family's motorcade. As a five-year-old, I sat on my dad's broad shoulders and cheered and waved my paper flag as the king and queen's ensemble passed by.

I was born in 1961, and was the youngest member of our family. I was often compared to my counterpart, the crown prince, as we were only four months apart in age. The prince was the firstborn son of the Shah and his third wife, Queen Farah. His birth ensured the continuation of the monarchy and the Pahlavi regime. Prince Reza was named after his grandfather, the first Pahlavi dynasty king, Reza Shah, and was one day to be known as Reza Shah II.

When my mother was pregnant with me, my parents decided that if the baby were a son, they would name him after my Iranian grandfather, Jacob, who had passed away in 1958. But if they were to have a daughter, Mom would surprise everyone with a name of her choosing.

Soon after my birth at Varjavand Hospital in Tehran, surrounded by extended family and friends, my mother announced that I was to be named after England's Princess Anne. Her decision was immediately repudiated by the visitors, who told her that she couldn't have chosen a worse name for an Iranian girl. That is because Anne, in Farsi, is slang for a four-letter word beginning with *s* and ending in *t*.

She was disheartened by this new knowledge, but, with my father at her bedside in the maternity ward, her gaze fell on a *Life* magazine that her mother, Miriam, had recently mailed from England. The photo spread was titled "Jacqueline Kennedy, America's Newest Star, in Beauty and Fashion." The first lady of the United States, the president's elegant and glamorous wife, wore an ivory silk chiffon blouse with a fuchsia Chanel jacket and an A-line skirt by Dior, a pearl necklace, black pumps, and a pillbox hat, which had become the latest international fashion accessory.

Mom had always had a flair for fashion. Before she met Dad, she had worked part time as a sales consultant at one of Birmingham's largest department stores and had become a trusted advisor to customers. She admired the first lady for her elegance and intelligence, and suggested that they name me Jacqueline. My father liked the idea and was thrilled because Jacqueline is the feminine version of Jacque or my grandfather's name, Jacob. Thus, I was named in his memory and after the first lady of the United States.

CHAPTER 2

My Iranian Mothers

My privileged upbringing as the daughter of a university professor and his foreign wife, in the northern Tehran neighborhood of Yousefabad, was comfortable—and unusual. Growing up in Iran, my siblings and I were considered to be *doeragehs*. The Farsi term refers to a person whose parents are from two distinct nationalities.

A desired trait in the Persian culture, such children were perceived to be a blend of the best characteristics of the East and the West. Their families were part of the educated elite who had had the opportunity to travel overseas and be exposed to Westerners. In the royal family, there were two doeragehs; the Shah's firstborn, Princess Shahnaz, from his first wife, Egyptian Queen Fawzia, and the Shah's second wife, Queen Soraya, who had Iranian and German roots.

But my family was also a rarity within our community. In a predominantly Shia Muslim nation, the small Jewish community of around one hundred thousand made up about one-third of one percent (that is, 0.29 percent) of the population of thirty-five million of that time. In my father's generation, marrying across continents among the Jewish community was a practice that was unheard of and simply not done. Therefore, as a Jewish doeragreh in a Muslim society, I was a minority within a minority.

Every weekday morning, Dad dressed meticulously in a suit and tie before he left home for work. In a Middle Eastern country where education was highly regarded, my father was respected as a professor at two prestigious universities. He taught metallurgy (a branch of science that studies the nature of metallic elements) at the Elm-o-San'at University (Iran University of Science and Technology) and at Tehran Polytechnic, which was the first established technical university in Iran. Both were regarded as prestigious engineering establishments of higher education. In Persian culture, holding an advanced degree was highly prized, and, therefore, my father, who had two advanced degrees in chemical engineering and meteorology, was shown respect wherever we went. Strangers would lower their heads and call him *ostad* (professor).

In addition to teaching, Dad worked part time for Habib Elghanian, the prominent Iranian Jewish businessman. Dad oversaw quality control of the metal items under production, among other duties. Twice a week, Dad put his second degree to use and worked at the meteorology office at Mehrabad International Airport. He drew charts, analyzed weather patterns, and prepared reports for the flight dispatcher and the pilots so that they were able to take off, fly, and land safely. Fluent in English, Dad could communicate directly with pilots of international airlines. Victoria and I once went to his office and stared in awe as he spoke to foreign pilots on the receiver.

My paternal family was originally from Isfahan, in central Iran, where my dad and his two siblings were born. My father's family had relocated to the capital city of Tehran years before my birth and had families of their own. The city's Jewish community was assimilated into society as a whole, and, therefore, my generation did not use the Judeo-Persian dialect of the tight-knit Jewish community of Isfahan and the few others like it across Iran, and so it has been lost.

My maternal family was originally from London, where my mom and her older brother were born. Because of the London Blitz during World War II, my mother's family relocated to Birmingham when she was a child. Mom's parents and Uncle Philip and his family lived on another continent, whereas my friends lived near their extended maternal families, visited back and forth, and celebrated holidays together.

Every weekday morning, a chauffeur in a company car with the airport logo arrived at our home to take Mom to her job with British Airways at

FIG. 3. My mother, Stella Lavi (*left*), with a coworker at Mehrabad International Airport, Tehran, 1973.

Mehrabad International Airport. As always, she looked elegant and stylish in her uniform, which included an identification badge and a matching tote. Mom held a high-powered position as the assistant to the airport manager. Because of Mom's job, our family received discounts on air travel. Therefore, we spent every summer vacation in England. Mom was committed to having us know her side of the family and experience life in England.

I referred to my mother as "Mom," while my friends referred to their mothers as "Maman." Their Mamans were competent homemakers, made elaborate Persian dishes, read Persian poetry, and had dark hair. My mom was not a homemaker, rarely cooked, did not know the Farsi alphabet (and thus, could not read anything in the language), and dyed her hair blonde (to match my own). Sometimes, Mom confused Farsi words, for example, intending "*sinie*" (tray) but saying "*sineh*" (a woman's breast). As a bilingual child, I constantly helped Mom by translating words and explaining cultural nuances. Despite her literary gaffes and limited fluency, Mom was well liked by everyone and treated with respect.

As my mother flourished in her Anglicized milieu at work, I relied on our household help to show me the Persian rules of engagement. In recent years, people from the poorer districts and rural areas on the outskirts of Tehran had flocked to the city in search of jobs and a better quality of life. Typically, they were less educated and less traveled, more traditional and more religious, and had larger families. They became our maids, gardeners, trash collectors, and the small-time vendors who pushed wheeled food carts through the city. On street corners, they peddled cooked red beets and hot fava beans in the winter, and walnuts soaked in salt water and grilled corn on the cob in the summer.

My family's four consecutive live-in maids showered me with love and affection, and because my mother was a career woman I spent a lot of time with them. Since I was sensitive and open by nature, I felt intimately connected to our maids, who were members of the tradition-bound underclass of Tehran. I listened to stories of their childhoods and large families. I considered each one to be my second mother. They were the ones who were fluent in all things Persian: the language, customs, history, and legends.

For example, before I learned it in school, Mahbobeh, our dynamic and imaginative live-in maid, would recite to me from the *Shahnameh,* the epic work of the Persian kings, written by eleventh-century Persian poet Ferdowsi. She told me about the great King Jamshid and how his arrogance was the cause of his downfall, and about Rostam, the son of Zal, and Rudabeh, a legendary warrior known for his fierce battles. In the more fanciful realm, Mahbobeh often repeated the story about a genie stuck in a bottle for thousands of years, who, upon gaining his freedom, granted a wish to his master.

While Mom would tell me about Cinderella, Mahbobeh would tell me the stories of the Persian queen Scheherazade. In order to save herself from death the next morning, as the king had wished for his previous queens, Scheherazade became the narrator of fascinating stories, keeping the king

FIG. 4. Me, age five, with a nanny in Tehran, 1966.

in suspense by ending each night's story at a critical juncture. In this way, the king had to keep his wife alive for another night to hear the rest of the story. This went on for one thousand and one nights. And then, King Shahryar changed his mind about killing his queen, and he and Queen Scheherazade lived happily ever after.

Through our maids, I also learned salutations and protocols of the Islamic faith and got a glimpse of their lifestyles. Buying fresh bread and groceries was a daily ritual, and I loved to go to the local markets with another live-in maid, Shamsi. When we walked through the busy streets of Tehran, she always held my hand tightly, her floral chador flapping in the wind. Shamsi's chador was a shapeless cloth sewn from a few yards of lightweight fabric, usually cotton or polyester. She wore it over her clothes, and it draped her body from the crown of her head to the floor. Shamsi held her chador in place by one hand at all times, as the large cloth swung from side to side with every step she took. When she had to search for the money in her wallet to pay for the groceries, she would use her teeth to hold on to the chador to prevent it from slipping down. The degree of a chador's coverage was controlled by the tightness of the wearer's grip. Many times, I observed a woman's chador slip backward and reveal her hair. This was not a cause for concern or embarrassment, at least not in Tehran and other urban areas.

The extent to which women covered themselves at that time was a choice. Iranian woman had been emancipated from wearing the hijab in 1936 by order of Reza Shah, the first Pahlavi monarch. The leader during my childhood, Mohammad Reza Shah, had eased the ban of hijab imposed by his father, and had left veiling as a personal choice for women to consider. Some women covered up to varying degrees, while others appeared in public like the women in the West. In our upper-middle-class northern Tehran neighborhood, women dressed in the latest Western fashions and never wore the chador. But our maids and women on the south side of the city and in smaller towns and villages had a different mind-set. They still chose to wear a chador in public as part of their usual, everyday outfit. Therefore, the sight of girls in miniskirts walking alongside women in light-weight chadors was a daily reminder of the contradictions in Iranian culture.

Shamsi and I went to the baker and the grocer, and I observed how she related to the shopkeepers. At the small neighborhood grocery shop, we exchanged our empty, washed bottles for fresh milk and sodas. Shamsi treated me to an ice cream cone with a gumball waiting in its point. At the *nanvayee* (bread shop) next door, we stood in line for the traditional, semi-rectangular, sesame-seeded *sangak* bread to come out of the oven. Its name is derived from "*sang*" (little stones), referring to the small stones on which the bread is baked in the *tanoor* (oven). Fresh, hot sangak bread spread with salty feta cheese and green herbs, such as basil, tarragon, and radishes (*sabzi khordan*), or with sour cherry jam, is the most delicious food imaginable.

Shamsi would sigh and say, "Unfortunately, Jacqueline *khanum* (Ms. Jacqueline), you don't have a mother who can teach you Persian etiquette. Your Mom gets away with not knowing the local customs because she is a *farangi* (a Westerner). But you are Iranian and must know how people expect you to act. For example, you should know the art of *ta'arof*, which is when a guest is offered peeled fruit from a large tray. You should always say, 'No, thank-you.' Then the hostess replies, '*Ghabel nadareh*' (I don't accept your refusal, it's nothing much), and only then you will take the fruit. To be polite, one must first refuse."

Another maid, Sadiqueh, was an excellent cook, although she herself, due to a medical condition, restricted salt from her diet and ate a tasteless, soft feta cheese. On the longest night of the year, we marked the winter solstice and welcomed the season with the festival of Shab-e Yalda. Sadiqueh would create a bountiful display of nuts and watermelon, symbolizing health, and pomegranate, symbolizing rebirth, on colorful hand-painted ceramic platters and in deep beveled-glass bowls. She taught me that I must eat watermelon, a summer fruit, on this chilly night to ensure that I "won't be cold in the winter and thirsty in the summer."

Sadiqueh had completed only a few years of elementary school, and it was my job to read aloud articles to her from her favorite weekly magazine. Through our conversations I learned about the opposing values that affected our daily lives, causing resentment and dividing Iran. The traditional sector of society from which she hailed disagreed with Iran's obsession with emulating the West. For example, I knew of families, especially American and other expatriates working for various companies in the city, who treated their dogs as treasured family members worthy of pampering. But Sadiqueh and her relatives considered dogs to be *najes* (unclean and untouchable) that had to be kept away.

I also noticed Sadiqueh's disdain for the movies shown at the theaters. In most movies, the representation of women as objects of desire, along with singing and dancing, were focal points of the Shah's conflict with the influential religious leaders and their followers. The clergy viewed the government's secularizing the people through the release of such movies as a plot to de-Islamize Iranian society and, therefore it declared cinema *haram*, or religiously forbidden.

But in spite of religious sanctions, cinema attendance grew. A favorite pastime of Iranians was to go and view the latest American imports. That is because the Pahlavi regime popularized the social aspects of Western, and particularly American, culture. The movies often depicted nudity, anathema to our cultural value of female modesty. Premarital sex was a common onscreen theme, which also runs counter to Islamic tradition.

Cinemagoers before the revolution mainly consisted of young men. Most women preferred to go to the movies accompanied by a male companion because some of the men harassed unaccompanied women and girls dressed in short skirts or short sleeves, at times engaging in unwanted touching and verbal incitements known as *matalak* in Persian. This occurrence wasn't widespread, but it wasn't uncommon either.

By the time I was in my early teens, I was particularly interested in our maid Farkhondeh's life. Farkhondeh was in a polygamous marriage, as her husband had two wives at the same time. The two women were referred to as each other's *havoo*. Farkhondeh's havoo took care of the house while she worked outside the home and helped with the finances. Farkhondeh had married at a very young age and looked older than her real age. She had rough hands from many years of menial housework in other people's homes, a hanging belly from the many children she had borne into this world, and sagging breasts from breastfeeding all those children. She would go back once a week to see her family, which included nine children. Farkhondeh's life was a stark contrast to the life that I had been accustomed to. Due to the family protection act, polygamy was uncommon and difficult to secure legally, but I knew that it did happen.

The class division between the wealthy and educated living in northern Tehran neighborhoods and the conservatives living in southern Tehran districts was getting deeper and more profound. Tehran had become a city of people divided by lifestyle and ideals, which gave way to an undercurrent of instability. Women's dress was evidence of the deep division between modernism and tradition across all sectors of society. As a teenager with deep Iranian roots, I felt the tremors of unease. I knew and loved citizens who belonged to two different worlds, separated by an uncrossable boundary.

CHAPTER 3

The Shah's Spectacular Parties

The Pahlavi royals had good reason to celebrate and throw spectacular parties with food, wine, dancing, and music. Iran was experiencing an idyllic, golden age of peace and prosperity. On October 26, 1967, Mohammad Reza Shah Pahlavi, who had reigned since 1941, was bestowed the title of Shahanshah (King of Kings) in an elaborate coronation ceremony. His third wife, the Shahbanou (Queen), was crowned "Empress Farah of Iran" during the formal event that was held at the Golestan Palace, which was the oldest of the royal complexes.

Our family watched the festivities on live television. Victoria and I snuggled between Mom and Dad on the sofa, and Raymond stood behind us. The six-year-old Crown Prince Reza, who was my age, sat beside his parents during the coronation ceremony.

The monarch sat on an ornate throne in the palace hall lined with mirrored walls and grand oil paintings of Persian art and the previous kings of Iran. A uniformed man approached the King of Kings and offered him a jeweled crown on a gold tray. The Shah raised the crown and placed it on his head. Dressed in white, covered with an embroidered velvet robe with a long train, Queen Farah walked down the hall, which was lined with nobility and officials. The Empress as well as the royal princesses dressed in long gowns of velvet, lace, or silk, accessorized with glistening tiaras, wore colorful sashes that draped from one shoulder to the opposite hip.

The queen knelt before the king, and another uniformed man offered him a second crown of a different design that, this time, was on a cushion. The Shah raised the second crown and placed it on his wife's head.

Following the coronation ceremony, the royal couple, followed by Crown Prince Reza, walked the length of the palace hall in long, slow strides and then rode in a horse-drawn carriage through the streets of Tehran. The jubilant crowds cheered "*Javeed* Shah!" (Long live the king) as the king raised his arm and waved to his subjects.

*

Four years later, in October of 1971, the King of Kings, Mohammad Reza Shah Pahlavi, hosted a five-day celebration that paid homage to Iran's prosperity and 2,500 years of monarchy in Iran.

Not only did this serve to link our King of Kings to Persia's first king, Cyrus the Great, but it also highlighted both monarchs' ethos of religious tolerance. As Jewish nationals of Iran, we felt proud that Cyrus the Great was revered in the Bible as the ruler who granted the Jews the freedom to remain in Persia. My community was able to trace back its roots in Iran for two and a half millennia. We were known as "Esther's children," referring to the Jewish holiday of Purim, which tells the story of a Jewish girl by the name of Esther who became the queen of the ancient Persian Empire. This holiday emphasizes her courage and heroism, having foiled the plot of the king's advisor Haman to destroy the Jewish people. Esther and her uncle Mordechai, who held a position inside of the king's court, are buried in Iran. Their mausoleum in the northern city of Hamedan is a revered place of pilgrimage for people of all faiths and a source of great pride for the Iranian Jewish community.

The celebrations were held in Takht-e-Jamshid, known as "Persepolis" in the West. This ancient city, which was once the ceremonial capital of the Persian Achaemenid Empire, is almost forty miles from the city of Shiraz, in southern Iran. Persepolis's architectural ruins offered an authentic backdrop, and its more remote location was easier for SAVAK, Iran's secret police and intelligence agents, to surveil and detain anyone who opposed the regime.

According to the broad media coverage, no expense was spared. Shiraz Airport was renovated, and trees were planted along the route between the airport and the luxury apartments that were built for our distinguished guests, six hundred foreign dignitaries who were world leaders and royals with their entourages. Top chefs were flown in from France to prepare each banquet.

Every evening leading up to the celebration, Dad would read the *Ettela'at*, the Persian daily newspaper in Farsi, and Mom would read the *Kayhan International* in English to follow the news. The long-awaited event finally arrived, and we followed every detail, televised for the world to behold. On opening day, the Shah and his queen greeted each guest with a handshake. Mom saw Prince Philip and Princess Anne and was overcome by nostalgia. She told Victoria and me about how lonely she was when she first arrived in Iran, unable to speak the language (she never did manage to master it) and without any friends. But by now, we had a large circle of friends, many of whom were foreigners living and working in Iran.

On day two of the national festivities, the featured entertainment was a parade of mock armies dressed in period costumes from the different eras of the Persian Empire. It was as if my thick history textbook came alive before my eyes. On the final day of the celebrations, the Shah and the Shahbanou paid homage to King Cyrus at the site of his mausoleum in Pasargadae.

Mom told me that the foreign press estimated that the extravagant expenditure of millions of dollars for the grand affair at Persepolis was speculated to have been the most expensive party in history.

I grew confused by the bold extravagance of the lavish, formal events. I knew about the poor districts on the south side of Tehran, and the two buses our maid Shamsi had to take when she returned to her family on the weekends. The 2,500-year celebration of the Persian Empire festivities was an Iranian event about our country's history, so I asked my dad, "Why were the foreigners having all the fun? Why were only a few Iranians invited? Why didn't they spend some of this money on the poor people?"

My dad reminded me that the Shah had already done plenty for the country and that we owed our comfortable lives to him. Our nation had an impressive ancient history, but before the Pahlavi era, Iran had a high illiteracy rate, a weak health system, neglected roads, and limited the rights of women and religious minorities. The father and son Pahlavi monarchs had made drastic reforms. Just thirty-six years prior, Reza Shah had initiated the greatest challenge of his era by abolishing the mandatory hijab (full body covering) for Iranian women.

"Jacqueline *joon* [dear], can you imagine covering your hair and your entire body whenever you step outdoors? Would you like to be told how to dress?"

"No, Baba joon. Obviously not. I like to choose my own outfits and leave my hair free."

"Today, we have a female minister of education, Dr. Farrokhru Parsa. She should be a role model for you. We have a rich country, and the Shah is showing the world how far Iran has come onto the global stage. You are a very lucky girl to have been born during these times."

We had commemorated a monarchy that had endured for two-and-a-half millennia, despite our country's many wars. We had celebrated the leadership of both the first and the current kings of Iran. The festivities were concluded with the dedication of the newly built Shahyad Tower (King's Memorial) in the center of Tehran. The imposing marble structure was strategically located near the Mehrabad International Airport, the symbolic gateway to the city. The first floor of the tower was the site of the new Museum of Persian History.

*

A few weeks later, I visited the tower and its museum with my classmates as a field trip from school. Most of my friends in the neighborhood, like Farideh, who lived across the street, attended public schools, but I went to Ettefagh Jewish day school, where Dad had once been the principal and a teacher. Dad loved his job but had to leave in 1957, when my family returned to England a few years before my birth. My father had been awarded a one-year fellowship through the World Meteorological Organization, funded by the United Nations and the Iranian government.

The Ettefagh school is still located in the center of the city, on Shahreza Avenue, the main thoroughfare, and across the street from the University of Tehran. Unlike most of Tehran's high schools, Ettefagh was coeducational. Known for its academic rigor, Ettefagh had a strong English curriculum with outstanding British and American educators. The student body of more than two thousand, in elementary through high school, represented

FIG. 5. My father, Rahmat Lavi (*standing, center*), principal and teacher at the
Ettefagh Jewish Day School, with students, Tehran, 1956.

all faiths (about 10 percent were not Jewish). The school had a synagogue
where anyone from any religion could voluntarily attend the short morning
service before classes began at eight o'clock.

Every morning, I looked forward to ten o'clock, when we, along with
seven million other students in the country, received free milk, fruit, and
cake, subsidized by the government. As mandated by the Department of
Education, we studied Arabic two hours per week. As a Jewish school, we
also studied Hebrew and Jewish studies for a few hours per week. During
religious and Hebrew studies, non-Jewish students had the option to stay
and learn or leave class. Because Ettefagh was an elite day school, we studied

a few hours of English as well as British and American literature every day, and everything else, such as science, math, biology, history, and Persian literature, was taught in Farsi. My school day ended at five o'clock. The weekend in Iran was only one day—Fridays; however, my school was closed Fridays and Saturdays (the Jewish Sabbath).

I was happy in school and had many friends, but I was closest to Nilofar and Yasmin. We spent most weekends at each other's houses. During recess, we laughed and played in the large school yard, and as we grew older, we sat for hours sharing our secrets and discussing the latest episode of *Donny & Marie*, the television variety show hosted by the American brother-and-sister duo Donny and Marie Osmond.

As Crown Prince Reza advanced to each higher grade in school, the educational system and curriculum for his new grade changed accordingly. Because I was the same age as the prince and in the same grade, I was a beneficiary of the new scrutiny placed on education. As the youngest child in my family, I was the only one to participate.

My textbooks were different from those used by my siblings, Raymond and Victoria, when they were my age. I studied contemporary mathematics, modern science, and vocational skills—all the better to contribute to a modernized Iran. For example, the middle school's sixth, seventh, and eighth grades were replaced by the first, second, and third grades of the new educational system known as *rahnamai* (showing the way). All schools—public and private—were obligated to comply with the new scholastic order.

Our heavy history books covered 2,500 years of kings and their dynasties. One heroic leader in our contemporary history class was Kemal Ataturk, the leader of Turkey, our neighbor to the west. In the 1920s and 1930s, Ataturk had modernized his country with the philosophy that secularism was the necessary feature of a progressive society. Our curriculum emphasized the idea of the separation of religion from politics. Personal beliefs of individuals were to be a private matter.

With the encouragement of my British teacher for English studies, on my own I studied for and passed the "O level," the General Certificate of Education Ordinary Level exam. The subject-based qualifications were identical to those taken by students in England. I took the tests in June 1975 and 1976 at the British Council in Tehran. With its British-appointed and local staff, the Council's priority was to provide English-language teaching and cultural events. My family and I enjoyed visiting the Council on a regular basis to watch the recent British feature films and English-language theatrical productions.

My experiences growing up in Iran were not that different from my Western counterparts. I went to friends' birthday parties, watched movies, traveled domestically and internationally with my family, read fashion magazines, and wore the latest Western trends: miniskirts or bell-bottom pants with fitted shirts and stylish dresses. Many small fashion boutiques lined the long and wide Pahlavi Avenue and other shopping districts.

Our own statuesque Queen Farah epitomized elegance and chic. In official portraits of the royal family displayed on the walls of our classrooms, banks, shops, and offices, I would admire her majesty's custom-made and designer outfits. Fashion magazines, such as the German language *Burda*, inspired the latest patterns for seamstresses and tailors to follow.

The most popular of the women's magazines, *Zan-e Rooz* (*Today's Woman*), which my sister, Victoria, read religiously every week, sponsored the Dokhtar Shayesteh pageant, which was the Iranian equivalent of Miss America. One year, Simin, a distant cousin of ours, was one of the twenty finalists and won first place in the category of Iran's best-dressed girl.

Young girls flocked to the beauty salons to recreate the hairstyles of the icons of the day, especially the Iranian diva Googoosh and the American sex symbol Farrah Fawcett. The first floor of the famous Kourosh department store was devoted to makeup and perfume counters and always packed with female shoppers. One of our second-floor tenants, Mrs. Nemati, a wife and mother who was educated as a nurse, dressed stylishly in silk blouses and pencil skirts and always wore high heels. When she stepped down the staircase, the scent of her French fragrance lingered in the air for hours.

*

The spring of 1977 marked many beginnings, festive and hectic, and even transformational. The two-week celebration of Nowruz, the Persian New Year, had begun. Nowruz is celebrated at the exact moment of the spring equinox. Iranians greet each other with "*Ayd-e-Shoma-Mubarak*" (Happy New Year), and enjoy the beautiful *haft seen* spread, a display of seven items that begin with the letter *s* in the Persian alphabet set amid tulips and hyacinths, and dine on the traditional holiday dish *sabzi polo* (white fish with dill, coriander, fenugreek, and parsley rice). The New Year holiday is concluded on the *sizdah* (thirteenth) day of the Persian month of Farvardin. It is customary to spend this day, known as *sizdah bedar*, with outdoor activities and a picnic.

In 1977 Passover started on the tenth day of Nowruz. The eight-day Jewish holiday of Passover commemorates the Israelites' exodus from Egypt. My birthday that year occurred during both the celebrated days of Passover and the celebration of Nowruz. I turned sixteen, and bonded deeply with many friends from diverse religious and cultural backgrounds who wished me happy holidays. I also developed a major crush on Elvis Presley.

Preparations for the spring holidays began weeks in advance. Known as *khaneh takani* (shaking the house), this was a time during which we scrubbed every nook and cranny and dusted from top to bottom. We took down the curtains and brought them to the dry cleaner and washed the windows until they sparkled. We bought new outfits and new shoes and were excited to have two weeks off from school. My main contribution was helping Mom with the desserts—replacing the pits in the large dates with walnuts. Mom would artfully arrange the sweets on silver trays and cake holders, heirlooms from my paternal grandparents, Jacob and Shoshana Lavi.

The first night of Passover, we hosted the traditional Seder meal for our extended Lavi family and close friends. The table was decorated with red, yellow, and white roses from our garden. Dad, dressed in a three-piece suit, presided over the service with the Haggadah, the book retelling the story of the Israelites' freedom from bondage in Egypt, and the blessings and meanings of the various, symbolic foods. Behind him, in the wall cabinet, was a framed photograph of Dad with the Shah, when his royal majesty visited his class at the university. A second photograph—of Granny Miriam, who had died a few months earlier in England—reminded me that she was with us in spirit.

The platters on the table presented a dizzying array of specialty foods, including large green onions; fresh mint and tarragon; grape leaves stuffed with rice and ground beef; grilled fish; roasted eggplant; saffron rice with barberry, slivered pistachios, and almonds; and *choresh fesenjan*, a stew made with chicken, walnut, and pomegranate paste and seeds. Best of all was the crispy golden *tahdig*, the crust of rice left to scorch on the bottom of the pan. Mom would make a separate meal for herself because, unlike my father's Sephardi custom, her Ashkenazi tradition prohibited eating rice on Passover and, also, she could not stand the sour taste of the dried lemons in the chicken entrée.

We ate and laughed and talked and, most of all, celebrated our freedom—then, in history, and now, in my people's home for the past 2,500 years. After the meal, we sipped tea and concluded the service with "Next year in Jerusalem," the traditional wish for our return to the land of Israel in the following year.

My cousin Kami joked in response that we already lived in the best place on Earth and had great lives. We had no reason to go anywhere. In full agreement and with no reason to doubt Kami's words, we all burst out laughing.

CHAPTER 4

Cracks along the Avenue

In the summer of 1977, I spent an unforgettable ten days at a Jewish camp in the coastal city of Ramsar on the Caspian Sea. On a hot, dry day, we left the crowded city of Tehran and drove four hours along winding roads to the lush, green, forested mountains of the countryside. Finally, we reached Mazandaran Province, with its vast tea plantations. The tribal women, in colorful layered skirts and large, brimmed hats, picked the tea leaves under the scorching sun. At a rest area, I talked to the locals and bought a few souvenirs.

At camp, I made many new friends and developed a special bond with a girl named Sima. We immediately clicked and had a lot in common. Over warm, thin sheets of fresh lavash bread and feta cheese, we talked about many things, especially the good looks of our counterpart, the crown prince; our schools; and our backgrounds. Although the camp was coeducational and activities were mixed, we were chaperoned by the counselors and, of course, had separate tents.

Our clique of boys and girls made sand castles decorated with seashells, ran into the waves, blasted the music of Greek singer Demis Roussos from our cassette players, and danced to the hit songs on the American music charts. In 1977, Elvis Presley's "Way Down" and "My Way" reached the top spots. At that moment, all I cared about was how hip I looked in my new polka-dot bikini; my cool, square sunglasses; and the latest craze—my red, platform sandals.

Back at camp, in the afternoons, we had arts and crafts and played card games in the air-conditioned cafeteria. In the evenings, my girlfriends and I sat on plaid, tribal kilims placed on the sand, and talked as the swoosh of the waves hummed in the background. Looking up at the sky, we would connect the stars to create animals and whimsical objects. Soon after, camp ended, and Sima and I promised to keep in touch.

*

By the time fall had arrived, and I became more self-assured about my multicultural identity (Iranian-born, half-English, and Jewish), a high school junior, and a grieving Elvis Presley fan (Elvis had suffered a heart attack and tragically died of acute respiratory distress at the age of forty-two in August 1977), my country was becoming more divided, and its contradictions starker. As I grew older in the late 1970s, I started to become more aware of what was going on around me. Nothing was as ideal as things had seemed at camp. Something different was brewing around me—at home, in the schools, and on the streets, but until then it had not impacted my life. By now I had become sensitive to the disparities in the culture, as the tensions that I sensed at home and in the schools were spilling out onto the streets. For instance, I recalled dining at fine restaurants on North Pahlavi Avenue and feeling the glares of waiters, doormen, and taxi drivers. Their stiff body language and blank facial expressions could not conceal their distaste for the Western values they felt were being imposed on the Iranian people.

Opposing values against the Pahlavi regime had increased among a broad sector of society. During my long lunch breaks, my friends and I would go to the local pastry shops and browse the bookstores that lined the south side of Shahreza Avenue. Sometimes, I would meet my sister, Victoria, who was studying at the university. In the cafeteria, I heard students, in hushed tones, express anti-Shah sentiments. I did not know if they belonged to a formal opposition group, but I was surprised to learn of their animosity for the Shah. Each espoused a plan for how the country could be better run without the current monarchy.

Two years earlier, in March 1975, the Shah had declared to a stunned nation the abolition of the multiparty system in Iran. The political replacement was a single legal party, known as the Rastakhiz (Resurgence) Party. A

FIG. 6. At age sixteen, Tehran, 1977.

year later, in March 1976, the Shah stunned the nation once again when he
replaced the Hijri Shamsi calendar, which is tied to the Prophet Mohammad's
migration from Mecca to Medina, with the Imperial calendar, dating to the
reign of King Cyrus. In one day, we went from the year 1355 to 2535. Our
maid, Farkhondeh, saw the mandate as an affront to her religion. Most
Iranians are Shia Muslims, a minority group among the larger population
of Sunni Muslims in the world.

Such decisions, which were enforced on the people against their will,
gave rise to the escalation of public animosity toward the Shah and his
establishment. Adding to these feelings was the fresh memory of the fall
of Dr. Mohammad Mosaddegh, Iran's prime minister in the early 1950s.
His government's most important policy was the nationalization of the
Iranian oil industry, which had been under British control for more than
forty years through the Anglo-Iranian Oil Company. During the 1953 riots
in Tehran, the Shah and then queen Soraya had fled the country. America's
Central Intelligence Agency (CIA), with the help of the British Secret
Intelligence Service (SIS), came to the aid of the Shah and organized a
coup against the prime minister. Mosaddegh, who was regarded as the
leading champion of secular democracy in Iran, was removed from power
and placed under house arrest. The Shah returned to Iran and established
himself as an autocratic ruler.

The tension in my country had evolved from petty resentment of the
Shah to a noticeable hatred of his absolute power and his feared secret
police, known as SAVAK. The efficiency of SAVAK ensured the survival of
the Shah's absolutist rule. Its informers could be anywhere, and they had the
authority to use all necessary means to arrest any dissidents. Furthermore,
this agency was notorious for its brutality and was viewed as the enemy of
the people and their desire for free democratic rule.

I had first heard about SAVAK as a child when my parents told me the
story of when the Shah invited King Frederick IX and Queen Ingrid of
Denmark to Tehran in 1963. Dad was on duty at the meteorology office.
Having studied the weather patterns, he directed the royals' pilot to divert the
plane to Beirut, Lebanon. The red carpet had already been rolled out, and the
welcome band was standing at attention. In Mom's reenactment, she raised
her voice and lifted her hand, "Who is this Mr. Lavi who has embarrassed his

Royal Majesty in front of the Danish king? How could he have been so bold as to prevent our distinguished guests from arriving on Iranian soil?"

General Esfandi, the head of airport security, was furious and summoned Dad for questioning. SAVAK agents, members of Iran's secret police and intelligence service, were also concerned that my father may have intended to embarrass the Shah or, worse, place him in jeopardy.

Dad explained that, according to the charts, due to hostile weather, it had not been advisable for the plane to land. Dad's forecast was again analyzed, and it was evident that he had been correct all along and had made the best decision.

This family story praised Dad's scientific acumen and professionalism, and also his courage having become the object of political suspicion. Dad cautioned me, "Do not get involved with politics. No matter who is in charge of the country, keep your thoughts to yourself and follow the authority. Play by the rules, Jacqueline, and you will benefit with abundance and good fortune. Be thankful for how we live."

*

However, more than the whispers of fringe political ideologies, I was alarmed by blatant, petty bigotry among students. One of Victoria's new friends, a posh girl named Neda, was curious why my sister and I "had foreign names." When we told her of our half-English parentage and Jewish roots, Neda said, "What a relief. I thought you might be Baha'i." Neda's disdain for Baha'is seemed like an outmoded throwback and a slur to all religious minorities in our modern secularized Iran.

The Baha'i faith, the largest non-Muslim religious group in the country, had been a traditional source of conflict within Iranian society. In the nineteenth century, Mirza Hussein Ali Baha, later known as "Baha'ullah" (glory of God), declared himself as the founder of the Baha'i faith. This contradicts the belief that the prophet of Islam is the last messenger of God. I admired the values of my Baha'i friends' faith, which include unity of all peoples, equality between men and women, and an emphasis on education.

The country's race to modernity—funded by our vast oil resources— did not feel authentic to me. And so, I continued to be finely attuned to the growing discontent that I witnessed.

FIG. 7. Me, at sixteen, on horseback in the English countryside, 1977.

*

The cultural divide became more pronounced on the Western New Year's Eve of 1978. I stayed home while Mom and Dad were at a friend's house. I turned on the television to watch the lavish state dinner hosted by the royal family at the Niavaran Palace in Tehran for the U.S. president Jimmy Carter and First Lady Rosalynn Carter.

The Shah rose to speak.

> It gives the Shahbanou and myself great pleasure to welcome you to our country. This reception is particularly auspicious since it takes place on the eve of 1978, and your presence here represents a New Year's gift for your Iranian friends. . . . Mr. President, you now have come to a country which has always had unshakable links with your country and your great nation. We are united together by a special relationship made all the closer by a wide community of mutual interests, which we share in our firm determination to contribute to the maintenance of world peace and security in assuring human progress and betterment.

Holding his champagne glass, President Carter gave the next toast:

> I would like to say just a few words tonight in appreciation for your hospitality and the delightful evening that we've already experienced with you. Some have asked why we came to Iran so close behind the delightful visit that we received from the Shah and Empress Farah just a month or so ago. After they left our country, I asked my wife, "With whom would you like to spend New Year's Eve?" And she said, "Above all others, I think, with the Shah and Empress Farah." So, we arranged the trip accordingly and came to be with you. . . . As we drove in from the airport this afternoon to the beautiful white palace where we will spend the night, and saw the monument in the distance, I asked the Shah what was the purpose of the beautiful monument. And he told me that it was built several years ago, erected to commemorate the 2,500th anniversary of this great nation. This was a sobering thought to me. We have been very proud in our Nation to celebrate our 200th birthday, a couple of years ago. . . . I was particularly impressed with a brief passage

from one of Iran's great poets, Sa'adi . . . 'Human beings are like parts of a body, created from the same essence. When one part is hurt and in pain, others cannot remain in peace and quiet. If the misery of others leaves you indifferent and with no feeling of sorrow, then you cannot be called a human being.' . . . The cause of human rights is one that also is shared deeply by our people and by the leaders of our two nations.

The president put down his drink and continued: "Iran, because of the great leadership of the Shah, is an island of stability in one of the most troubled areas of the world. This is a great tribute to you, Your Majesty, and to your leadership and to the respect and the admiration and love which your people give to you."[1]

I was amused by the effusiveness of the president's words. President Carter had not walked the streets of Tehran like I had. He had not ridden in a taxi and listened to the driver's complaints. He had not had lunch with University of Tehran students expressing anti-Shah rhetoric. Iran was not an "island of stability" (as Carter had fawned), but a land of warring values poised on a fault line.

As much as I was aware of the contradictions around me, I had the privilege of belonging to another culture: that of my mother's family. Every year, I spent the long summer months with my relatives in England. Once there, I assimilated into the society as an English girl who lived in Iran for some part of the year.

CHAPTER 5

England

In the summer of 1978, I had finished my junior year at Ettefagh. My friends from school and camp met regularly at Farah Park, movie theaters, and the Jewish youth club, and so this summer, unlike the previous years, I wanted to stay in the city and not go to England.

But Mom was experiencing a flare-up of recurring back pain and needed me to accompany her to England for a second medical opinion. I whined to my parents that I didn't want to go to England, that I wanted to stay and enjoy the city, and that I had to study for the *konkoor* (the Iranian university entrance exam).

My brother, Raymond, had followed in our Dad's footsteps and left Iran to pursue his education in England on graduating from high school in 1970. Raymond and his English wife, Christine, had been married for two years and had a two-month-old baby girl, Emily. My sister, Victoria, had also married, and she and her Iranian husband, Cyrus, had a twelve-month-old baby girl, Leila, who was born in England a year before.

My parents insisted that, unlike prior years when I had spent every summer vacations in England, this trip would be short so that I could get back to my social life in Tehran. Dad had already booked a checkup and medical care for my mom at a private hospital in London. He was unable to leave work, and my sister had her hands full as a student, wife, and mother. I, on the other hand, wasn't going to start school for another six weeks.

Mom continued, "I will have physical therapy sessions and then stay with Raymond and Christine in Coventry for some time. You will be able to return home in a few weeks. What do you expect will happen while you're away? Let me guess. All your friends will drop everything and leave the country. Everything will be shut down. And the whole nation will turn upside down in your absence."

I laughed at Mom's sarcasm, her scenario of my social set in an Iran run amok. She was right, how could anything be different upon my return? My friends, my school, my community, and the city were not going anywhere. I would be back in time to enjoy the rest of the summer with my friends and to prepare for my senior year.

*

A few days later, Mom and I were on a Pan Am flight to London. Raymond and Christine and my uncle Philip and his family met us at Heathrow.

Mom was admitted to the medical center in London for tests and bed rest, and I was to remain near to be of comfort to her. School would not start for many weeks. By train, bus, and tube, I shuttled between Raymond and Christine's two-story home in Coventry, Uncle Philip and Aunt Gertrude's home in Birmingham, and Mom's hospital room in London.

I spent each weekend with Philip and Gertrude and their three daughters. My aunt's dishes of matzah ball soup followed by brisket and potato kugel, roast beef tartlets, and fish and chips were a different culinary experience than Persian cuisine. My cousins and I would play Uno, a card game, and, in the backyard, badminton. We would talk about the latest movies and giggle all night. Sometimes we went to London together. After visiting Mom, we watched the changing of the guards at Buckingham Palace, fed the pigeons in Trafalgar Square, and visited the London Zoo.

I missed Granny Miriam and Grandpa Murray, who had both passed away. Grandpa Murray had died when I was a toddler, but Granny Miriam's memory was fresh in my mind, as she had been gone for only a year. My grandmother was the only grandparent that I ever knew, as my paternal grandmother, Shoshana, had passed away when I was an infant. Granny Miriam and I were close, and we used to have long conversations about life on both sides of the ocean. On our family's annual visits to England,

FIG. 8. Me, at seventeen, seated on a motorbike, Coventry, 1978.

I would accompany my grandmother to her friends' social gatherings. I remained quiet as she proudly bragged that this granddaughter of hers, who looked like any other Jane or Mary, could speak fluently in a foreign language (meaning Persian) that wasn't French or German.

Uncle Philip told me stories of World War II, when the family lived through the London Blitz. Britain had declared war on Germany, and German bombers blasted London day and night. My uncle told me how he would draw the thick curtains across the windows when the sirens wailed. He would then explain that during an aerial bombing, one had to conceal any light from the bomber jets above. The family would go under the stairs or take cover in a brick bomb shelter in the street. Finally, my mother's family moved to their new home in Birmingham, but it wasn't that much safer.

"Our Stella, your mother, was about twelve years old. Once, Stella came home telling us how surprised she and her classmates were to have a man of about thirty as their teacher. He had some heart ailment, exempting him from fighting in the army."

My uncle had been awarded a medal for bravery for his actions during the war. He had joined the Home Guard after Prime Minister Churchill's remarkable speech to the House of Commons on June 4, 1940. He would often reenact the prime minister's famous quote: "We will fight in the streets, we will fight on the beaches, and we will never surrender."

At the age of eighteen, my young and brave uncle was guarding the entrance of a factory that produced Bakelite, a unique material used in various kinds of wartime equipment. That was the main reason why the Germans targeted and bombed the facilities. Uncle Philip managed to move a few innocent passersby out of harm's way before the gates fell over him. He was buried under the massive iron bars for a long time before he was rescued. He had to undergo many surgeries to align his mangled leg.

Finally, on D-Day (June 6, 1944), my mother's family sat nervously around the radio, listening to the reports about the Normandy landings. Soon after, the Germans and the Japanese surrendered, and World War II ended. My uncle Philip told me how they celebrated with block parties and how the joyous children banged on metal dustbin lids.

My uncle's renditions of his war life were a far cry from my comfortable life in Tehran. I couldn't imagine what being in a war and bombed from above would feel like.

*

During the week, I helped out with my niece, Emily, and befriended some teenagers in the neighborhood. I also spent my time shopping, taking horseback riding lessons, and writing long letters to Sima, my best friend from camp. My favorite pastime, though, was reading under the branches of the red oak tree in my brother's backyard.

One beautiful August Sunday, over breakfast, Raymond hollered, "Savages!"

I looked up in surprise.

Raymond continued reading the morning paper, "Four hundred and twenty people were burnt to death in a fire that was deliberately set ablaze at Cinema Rex in Abadan—about four-hundred miles south of Tehran."

"What are you talking about? Did you say 'deliberately'?"

"It says here that 'men barred the doors and doused the place with gasoline before setting it alight.' Did you hear me? The exit doors were locked from the outside, trapping the people inside. They don't know who did it. No one has claimed responsibility. This is horrendous."

"Poor people! How could this have happened?"

"They were watching *Gavaznha* [*The Deer*, the title of a movie]. It must've been *Bambi* or the like."

"I know the movie *Gavaznha*. It's a modern Iranian film—not a kid's movie."

The magnitude of the terror was very upsetting and hard to fathom. People flocked to air-conditioned theaters during the intense summer heat of southern Iran. Although no one had claimed responsibility, I knew that the inferno was an act of rebellion against the Shah. I consoled myself that although horrific, the blaze had happened in Abadan, far away from our home in Tehran.

*

I still had several weeks before school would start. On a quiet evening in early September, I sat on the couch watching my favorite TV show, the American soap opera *Dallas*. What was J. R. Ewing scheming this time? The phone rang, and Christine answered.

"Oh, hello, Victoria. How are you keeping up with Leila? Is she walking yet? We are all fine. Emily is almost two months old. Yes, Jacqueline is here. She has been a great help to us. Jacqueline has become an expert in preparing the bottle. Rubin, Myrna, and the girls [my mother's cousin and his family] visited last weekend from Manchester. Andrea and Jacqueline have a lot in common. No, Raymond has gone out to get some milk for the baby. It's just Jacqueline and me here watching the telly. Yes, I'll put her on."

I got up and complained, "Why does everyone want to talk at the critical moment in the show? There are four commercial breaks in one hour, but I have to get up now."

"Hi, there. What's up? How's Dad? Mom was concerned if the maid has cleaned the cabinet under the sink. How is Leila? I miss her so much. Is she talking yet?"

Victoria's voice was quiet and tense. "Jacqueline, listen to me. Don't come back. I can't say much over the phone, but things are rapidly changing here. There have been shootings at Jaleh Square [in Tehran]. It is rumored that a few thousand people were killed and wounded yesterday in riots against the. . . ."

"What are you talking about? I don't understand. School starts in two weeks."

"Dad agrees. I can't say much over the phone. The Jewish community is alarmed. It's not easy to make international calls. I'll try and call again. Goodbye, Jacqueline."

I hung up the receiver, stunned. Victoria and Dad wanted me to stay put for a while and not come home. Didn't President Carter and Rosalynn just celebrate New Year's Eve with the Shah and Queen Farah in Tehran—praising our "island of stability"? What was happening? I scoured the newspapers but did not find much. Reporting on events in a faraway Middle Eastern country was hardly headline news to the average reader in England.

On my next visit to Mom at the rehabilitation center in London, she tried to allay my fears by telling me that we were established in Tehran. We couldn't just pick up and leave because of some upheaval. The sketchy event that occurred in September 1978, the one Mom referred to as "some upheaval," became known as "Black Friday," when government tanks and helicopters opened fire against thousands of protestors in Tehran.

During the next few days, we remained in limbo. We were no clearer on the situation, and calling home was difficult. Once able to connect, we spoke with caution, assuming our conversation was being monitored. My father was helping my brother financially, so my staying would not be an economic strain on him and his family. I valued my independence and knew that I would leave at the first opportunity. The next day, I went to a local high school and inquired about enrolling. Since I had taken two O-levels, transferring credits would be easier.

I was excited about my new prospects, and that evening I stayed up in the living room and watched the programming on late-night television. During a commercial break, I got up and opened the door to walk down the narrow hallway to go to the kitchen and make myself a cup of hot chocolate. As I opened the door of the living room, which was close to the bottom of the staircase, I heard hushed voices. In the dark hallway, I saw the outlines of Raymond and Christine standing at the top of the stairs. I heard my name, so I moved back and remained by the side of the hallway wall, listening to their conversation.

My brother said, "Jacqueline needs to stay. I don't know what is going on over there, but whatever it is, it doesn't look good."

His wife said, "No, let her go. I don't want her to stay here."

Raymond pleaded, "Let her stay for a few more weeks, and we'll see if the situation changes. My father will provide her with the means to find a dorm or another place to stay. We also have other relatives here. Her stay here with us is temporary."

Christine said, "No. Send her back. I don't want her to stay here."

My knees weakened as I gasped for air. They were arguing about my future. Given how I was helping with the baby and the house, I had no idea I was considered to be in the way. Deeply saddened and hurt, I was too proud to tell anyone what I had overheard.

The next day, I received a letter from Sima in Tehran. Her tone was optimistic, with no hint of anything out of the ordinary. She wrote, "Jacqueline, come back soon. The flower shop at the corner of Kourosh department store [where we had always met] is waiting for us. Where are you, girl? I miss you. Come back soon."

I began to console myself that things might not be that bad back home. The opposition to the Shah would be crushed, and I had one more year of high school. I traveled to England every summer, so maybe it would be better for me to leave for Iran now and return as soon as I graduated.

A few days later, Raymond drove me to Heathrow. I sat silently in the front passenger seat. Christine stayed home.

PART 2

Fear

1978–1979

CHAPTER 6

Homecoming

Mehrabad International Airport was a ghost town. The silence was eerie, and the air felt solemn and heavy. At 1:30 a.m. it was supposed to be quieter than usual, but this was not a typical calmness. I collected my luggage and entered the reception area. Where were the usual large, cheering crowds of relatives and friends? Where was Dad, who, at six-foot-two, was usually the easiest to spot? And Victoria and Cyrus? I gasped. No one is here, except for roving, uniformed soldiers in heavy black boots and with rifles on their shoulders. I had only seen armed militiamen in the movies. What is going on here?

I warily followed the other passengers down the stairs and to the curb. The hot night air hit me in the face. A soldier pointed at me and said, "You! Get into this taxi and move as fast as you can. You can't linger here. Move!"

I shrunk into the back seat as the taxi driver spoke to the soldier, who was now reviewing my passport and travel documents. He returned my papers to me and handed the driver a yellow permit.

The city of a few million inhabitants was empty. It was as if there had been an alien invasion and all the citizens had been taken away. Where is everyone?

"You look confused, Ma'am. Haven't you heard?"

"What? Why is everything so desolate? Where are the people? What has happened?"

"Everyone is inside their homes or another building. Tehran is under martial law, as are a few other cities in Iran. No one is allowed to leave their homes and be on the streets during the evening without special permission. Otherwise, they will be shot."

We approached a checkpoint, and a soldier said, "*Eist* [Stop]."

At the command, the driver hit the brakes and rolled down the window. Politely, he said, "*Mosafereh* [She is a passenger]."

After reviewing my travel documents, the soldier turned toward the driver, "Open the trunk!" He searched my belongings and then said, "You are clear. Go."

During the thirty-minute ride home, we were stopped at two more checkpoints, questioned, the trunk searched, and released.

At home, the staircase lights were on. I heard Dad's footsteps rush down the stairs to open the door. "Jacqueline *joon,* you are finally home. I was so worried about you and felt so helpless not being able to come and get you at the airport."

*

The next day, I went out to buy school supplies and window-shop along Pahlavi Avenue. It was pandemonium. The traffic was heavy with honking cars, and the diesel fumes were suffocating. The sidewalks were packed with pedestrians. Street vendors were hollering. I missed the tranquility of the English countryside, the large oak tree in the backyard of Raymond's house and the smell of the freshly cut grass in the front.

I also missed how punctual English buses were. I jumped on the next bus that screeched to a halt. I found a seat at the rear by an open window. I noticed scratches on the back of the seat that I faced and froze in horror: "*Marg bar Shah* [Death to the Shah]."

My body began to shake. What if someone thought that I had written this? I would be taken away, imprisoned, and tortured. In written form, the Shah was referred to as "His Majesty," "His Royal Highness," and "the King of Kings." Not only was the graffiti using a taboo moniker but also wished death upon him! Never before had I seen such language in plain view. Trying to appear calm and avoiding eye contact with anyone, I got up and pushed through the passengers standing in the aisle at the front. I counted the minutes until the next bus stop, where I could jump off.

The news in the capital city and around the country only seemed to get worse. There were strikes against private-sector businesses and government-owned industries. A high-ranking cleric named "Ayatollah Khomeini" had become the symbol of unity for the opposition and the leader of the downtrodden. I knew that the Ayatollah had previously denounced the Shah's close ties to America and his modernization programs, known as the "White Revolution" (Enqelab-e Sefid). In 1963, the Ayatollah led three days of riots, and a few hundred people were killed. He was sent into exile in Iraq. Fourteen years later, he was expelled from Iraq and granted political asylum in France.

The Ayatollah's influence as a political renegade was belied by his image— that of a kind, elderly grandfather. From his humble accommodation in a Paris suburb, the Ayatollah's sermons were broadcast on foreign Persian-speaking radio stations. Leaflets with his instructions and cassettes of his lectures were distributed on the streets of Tehran and other cities. The campaign was effective, inciting anti-Shah riots and demonstrations. Burning rubber tires, and the resulting thick, black smoke and acrid smell, became the preferred means of mass protest.

School had started, but I knew that each day I left the house at my own risk. The main topic of conversation among students was our concern over the political situation, who was leaving the country, and if and how we, too, should leave. A few weeks later, my high school, along with many other institutions and organizations, was shut down.

I felt like I was playing a never-ending game of musical chairs, the children's game where there is iteratively one less chair than the number of players. The winner is the one who sits in the last chair in the last round when the music stops. The loser is the child left standing. I was unseated at the airport when I arrived, and no family was there to meet me and drive me home. I abandoned my seat on the bus when I saw the graffiti. And now even my school desk was pulled out from under me. I went home that afternoon and stayed.

*

I was glad that Mom was still in England, recuperating. I did not want her to return to the volatility in Iran. Victoria and Cyrus shared my concerns, but Dad, as always, remained loyal and optimistic. He kept repeating, "The Shah is invincible. He has remained in power for the past thirty-seven years, through occasional protests and even riots. Worst case, he has an heir. The Crown Prince Reza is almost an adult. As long as the King of Kings remains in the country, we remain in the country and are safe."

Dad also reminded me of the last unsuccessful assassination attempts on the Shah, in 1949 and 1965. He said again how our Jewish roots in the country went back for more than two-and-a-half millennia. Furthermore, the elderly cleric (meaning the Ayatollah) had stirred up trouble in the past, and he would be crushed again. According to Dad, "This too shall pass."

CHAPTER 7

When Jacqueline Met Ebi

In late October 1978, Mom was still in England. I sat at my desk to write her a letter. She had left the rehab center and had spent time with Raymond, Christine, and the baby. She was more than ready to come home. I had strongly advised Mom not to return to Tehran, but she was eager to reunite with her husband and the rest of the family. Like Dad, Mom believed that the disruptions were an inevitable part of life in the Middle East, and things would eventually return to normal.

Dad was in the garden, enjoying his pipe and admiring the roses. As he entered the room, the telephone in the foyer rang, and we both walked over to answer it. Dad handed me a dozen white, yellow, and red roses and picked up the receiver.

"Hello? Hi, Darius. How are you? How is the family?"

"Who? Where? Isfahan? The couple with the baby boy? Ah, yes, now I remember. My goodness, has it been that long? This afternoon? Oh, alright. We will see you soon. Goodbye."

"Baba joon, what did Uncle Darius [Dad's brother] say? Who is in Isfahan?"

"We are going to have visitors this afternoon."

"Now? Who? We don't know anyone still in Isfahan. You haven't been back in years, and Raymond, Victoria, and I have never been there."

"When I returned to Iran after studying in England, where I had met your mother, my parents hosted a welcome home party for me in Isfahan. The large, wooden front door was left ajar, and people kept coming in. In those days, overseas travel was an adventure not accessible to most. I was one of the few who not only had gone abroad but also had attained higher education. Everyone wanted to hear my stories about *farang* [the West, referring to Europe and America] and how people lived on the other side of the world. I was overwhelmed by their sincerity. Aziz, a close friend of my brother, your uncle Darius, arrived with his wife, Malka, and their two sons—a toddler and, in Malka's arms, a chubby eight-month-old. Aziz had a distinguished, short, stubby mustache. Malka was taller than the average Iranian women and had a fair complexion. If I didn't know better, I would've mistaken her for a European lady. The older son ran off to play with the other children. While we were speaking, the baby gurgled and babbled constantly. Goo goo. Ga ga."

"Baba joon, you have such a good memory."

"Well, the baby had gorgeous green eyes and was cheerful and sociable. He smiled at me, and when I picked him up, he held onto my pinkie and continued to babble on. Then Aziz said something I would never forget."

"What?"

"Aziz said, 'I believe our baby will make us proud by becoming the Rahmat Lavi of our family.' Over the years, I have asked Darius how Aziz and his sons are doing. A few years ago, Darius told me the baby, named Ebi [short for Abraham], had been accepted into a seven-year medical school program. I felt proud, remembering his father's words."

"Baba joon, your story is lovely, but frankly, I couldn't care less. What does all this have to do with the phone call?"

"Uncle Darius said that the mother, Malka, is in town from Isfahan, visiting her daughter who is married and settled in Tehran. She doesn't live far from us, and they want to come and show their respect and introduce the daughter. We could be a source of support for her and her husband. It's for a good cause."

"Today? I look terrible. I don't know these people, and I'm not in the mood to entertain."

"Jacqueline, your mother is not here. Sit for a little while. I'm sure they won't stay long. The maid left an hour ago, and no one else is here. Now, go and wash and prepare some fruit. There are also dates and cookies in the cabinet."

I gave back the roses to Dad to arrange in a tall beveled-crystal vase. I shrugged my shoulders and reluctantly went to the kitchen to wash some fruit. Dad called after me, "It's always better to avoid conflict and to open our house to guests. I'm sure they won't stay long."

Soon, the doorbell rang, and I peeked through the corner of the curtain. Uncle Darius and two women, stylishly dressed, were at the front door. The older woman looked to be in her early fifties and wore a navy-and-white floral dress. With well-defined cheekbones and a fair complexion, she was strikingly beautiful. The younger woman had long light-brown hair and wore a navy skirt and a cream silk blouse with a large shawl over her shoulders.

"*Befarmayed. Chosh amadid.* [Please come in. Welcome.] Thank you for the *gaz.* [A white pistachio-filled nougat from Isfahan]."

I also came forward and directed our guests to the living room. Uncle Darius introduced us and said the short notice was because Malka had to return to her city the next morning. I remained silent and listened to the conversation, mostly about the people Dad had known in his youth in Isfahan.

Then Malka said, "Mr. Engineer Lavi, it is such a pleasure to see you again after so many years. Aziz also sends his regards. He hopes to see you in person sometime soon."

"I remember meeting you and your husband at my parents' home when I returned to Iran so long ago. You had two children then, and I held the baby."

"Yes, time does go by fast. Ebi is now a second-year general surgery resident at Pahlavi University in Shiraz."

"*Mashallah* [an expression of praise meaning 'God has willed it']. His accomplishments are impressive."

Malka turned toward her daughter, "This is Haleh. She is married and lives in Tehran. Aziz and I visit her as often as we can. We are concerned about her in the big city during these difficult times. I hope you will keep an eye on her, and it would be wonderful to have friends nearby."

"Of course. My wife, Stella, is in England and will return soon. My older daughter, Victoria, is married and lives close by. Jacqueline is in her last year of high school, but all schools have been shut down."

I was getting tired of all this friendly banter. I wanted our guests to leave so I could relax and watch *Rangarang*, the musical variety show, on television.

*

Soon after, Haleh reciprocated with an invitation for lunch at her home. Her parents were in town, and other former Isfahanis now living in Tehran, who Dad also knew, would be there. Mom would also go with us. She had returned to Iran and was overjoyed that her health was restored and to be home. It seemed as if the more other people tried to escape the country's chaos, the more entrenched my family became. Obviously, we were not going anywhere. Mom "just got home," and Dad kept saying, "This, too, shall pass."

The chaos continued to escalate. The nexus of the conflict was the Shah himself. To mark the fourteenth anniversary of Ayatollah Khomeini's exile to Iraq, November 4, 1964, students at the University of Tehran gathered, and some tried to pull down a statue of the Shah. In response, the army fired into the crowd of young rebels. Until then, I had associated military tanks with distant battle scenes, but now they were parked along the streets of Tehran, and from them soldiers were firing on unarmed civilians.

The next day, hundreds of thousands of people demonstrated in Tehran and set fire to businesses associated with the West and imperialism; foreign banks and the British embassy were targeted. Later that day, the Shah made a televised speech to the nation. Dressed in a suit and tie, he looked weary as he spoke into three microphones. I hung on every word and then translated the details to Mom. "I once again repeat my oath to the Iranian nation to undertake not to allow the past mistakes, unlawful acts, oppression and corruption to recur but to make up for them. . . . I have heard the revolutionary message of you the people."[1]

I became deeply concerned about the future of the country with the last sentence of the King's speech, "I urge the young generation to whom our country belongs to not to burn down our homeland. Let us all think about our beloved Iran. Let us think about Iran and its future." Never had I seen the Shah look so defeated or heard him plead with the people. I knew that this was the end for the man who had taken for himself the title Shahanshah (King of Kings) and Shahbanou for his empress.

Ayatollah Khomeini urged the people to continue staging mass demon-strations and strikes. The Ayatollah garnered broad support across many sectors: the urban poor, university students, trade unions, intellectuals, leftists, and Islamists. They believed the Shia cleric's promise: utopia. A utopia where a woman could dress as she pleases, where people would be able to choose a democratic government. A country that would be free of Western intervention. A nation personified by its divine principles.

No one questioned how this would be possible. A leading slogan at the time, appearing on walls and banners and in revolutionary songs was, "Only when the devil departs, the angel will arrive."

The Shah was cast as the devil, and the Ayatollah was the angel.

*

Dad, Mom, and I arrived at Haleh's home, and we were introduced to Ebi, the once babbling baby now in residency training in Shiraz, six hundred miles south of Tehran. Since the country had come to a near standstill, and most institutions were on strike, Ebi was able to take a break from his grueling schedule and join the family in Tehran.

I was impressed with Ebi's accomplishments, mannerisms, and body language. He wore a camel sweater and cream pants, a dark-brown leather jacket, and a leather belt and tan shoes. He was handsome (those gorgeous green eyes!) and well educated, but not arrogant. He sat with confidence and had a quick sense of humor. He delighted the children with card tricks and spoke respectfully to our elders. My father observed Ebi, too. Was he, as his father had predicted, the Rahmat Lavi of his family? Dad and Ebi were both self-made men who had beat the odds and created bright futures for themselves.

A few days later, Ebi and I had our first date. Before I left the house, Mom gave me some advice, "Sit confidently. Remember to keep your shoulders back and your chin up."

At Chattanooga Restaurant on North Pahlavi Boulevard, Ebi and I sat facing each other. I tried to balance my posture with crossed legs. Our café glacés arrived in tall glasses, accompanied by chocolate éclairs. Ebi and I talked for a long time, and I got to know more about him. He told me that he had studied French in high school and continued advancing his language skills in college. At the beginning of his second year of residency training in Shiraz, a visiting professor from France had invited him to spend six months of the five-year residency training in Paris. He had returned only last September, amid the upheaval in Iran.

In response, I told him that I also had been away in England, and had returned to Iran in late September. It was a well-known fact that Pahlavi University was the most esteemed university in Iran and conducted its courses in English. Therefore, I was confused as to how he studied there. He explained that although his English had improved, the majority of his readings were primarily in technical English that most native speakers wouldn't necessarily understand either. Pahlavi University had a reciprocal program with the University of Pennsylvania in the United States that would recognize his degree once he had completed the residency training within the next few years. This meant a lot to him because, given the political situation in Iran, it was good to know that he would have the option to start a new life in the United States.

Ebi was intelligent and well traveled. I also learned that he was a member of the college chess team and played tennis. He mentioned the annual Jashn-e Honar Summer Art Festival, which was held in Shiraz. "The festival showcases performing artists and musicians from around the world. This year, though, due to the street violence, the festival has been canceled."

"I have seen many of the performances on television."

"Maybe, one day, you will visit Shiraz."

*

Ebi and I continued our relationship by phone, and every few weeks he traveled to Tehran. In the meantime, the political turmoil continued. Torn, burnt photographs of the royal family littered the streets, and anyone could be arrested or sprayed with tear gas. Even staying home entailed risk. One day, our next-door neighbor Mahrookh khanum (Ms. Mahrookh) ran to our home screaming hysterically. She had been tending the stew on the stove when a stray bullet flew through the large front windows and whizzed above her head.

Demonstrators were antagonistic toward the West, especially the United States, which they referred to as *shaytan-e bozorg* (the "Great Satan"). Israel was *shaytan-e kochak* (the "Little Satan" or the "Zionist State"). Every day, the people were introduced to another cleric. Where had all these religious figures been before?

With the strengthening of the Shia clergy, religious minorities began to feel more insecure about their future in an Islamic republic. After the establishment of the Shia sect of Islam in Iran in the sixteenth century, their clergy had gained ultimate authority. Under their jurisdiction, the religious minority communities had been treated unfavorably, and this practice continued until the Pahlavi kings drastically reduced the clergy's influence.

I repeatedly heard slogans touting the religious path: "*Tanha rah-e saadat, shehadat ast*" (The only way to salvation is through martyrdom); "*Esteglal, azadi, Jomhuri-e Islami*" (Independence, freedom, and an Islamic Republic); "*Hezb faghat Hezbollah, rahbar faghat Ruhollah*" (The only government should be the government of God; and the only leader should be *Ruhollah*, which was Ayatollah Khomeini's first name).

In an attempt to appease the resistance, the Shah abolished the Imperial calendar and reverted to the Hijri Shamsi calendar. But it was too little, too late. The protestors, dressed in white to symbolize a death shroud, took to the streets again. They were ready to die.

CHAPTER 8

Nightly Calls of *"Allahu-akbar"*

The growing frenzy to overthrow the Shah was relentless. The Ayatollah had devised a plan for his followers to continue the fight. As instructed by the Ayatollah, every evening at 8:55 p.m., supporters turned off their lights and took to their open, flat rooftops or balconies. Then, at the stroke of nine, the city erupted in a roar. Loud and forceful, hundreds of thousands of people stood in the cold and shouted, *"Allahu-akbar.* [The Islamic phrase, in Arabic, means 'God is great.' In Farsi, God is referred to as *Khoda.*] Allahu-akbar. Allahu-akbar. Allahu-akbar." The ecstasy of dissent lasted about ten long minutes.

In the darkness, the protestors felt united, powerful, defiant, and a camaraderie with others like themselves who were trying to free the country and reach the promised land of an Iran free from the rule of the Shah. They looked up to Ayatollah Khomeini as a holy man of God. We turned out our lights, too, lest our home be a visible target and branded pro-Shah. Moreover, our family, Jewish, and with a mother from the "evil West," had to be even more vigilant. However, we never went to the roof. Dad said, "Certainly not. You want to cry out, 'Allahu-akbar'?" I nervously asked Mom, "What if our neighbors notice we weren't there?" Reasonably, Mom said, "Tell the neighbors to the right that we were standing on the left side of the rooftop, and tell the neighbors on the left we were standing on the right side."

Sometimes, Victoria, Cyrus, and Leila, now a toddler, would stay over. The six of us would sit quietly on the sofa in the darkened living room with the curtains drawn. Victoria's husband could not keep still. The eldest son of seven children of a wealthy textile importer in Tehran, and an architect by profession, Cyrus was analytical and cautious and felt responsible for his parents' well-being. Cyrus said, "What guarantee do we have that we are safe? Some people might take advantage of the situation, and loot shops and rob us in our homes."

Dad paused, holding his pipe, "Cyrus joon, this is an ideological revolution. It's not about money or comfort. The people want more autonomy."

Cyrus was not convinced, "I don't like the way things are going. It is better for us to leave everything behind and just go and be safe." Three of Cyrus's siblings had already left Iran and were living in Los Angeles.

Dad said, "Go abroad? To do what? Things will settle down somehow. They are not going to get their wish by turning to the clergy. Ultimately, they will lose more than they had had before."

Mom added, "It is like opening a Pandora's box. Who knows what will happen in the future?"

*

One evening, I stayed over at Victoria and Cyrus's house. The nightly calls of "Allahu-akbar" of their neighbors at the top of their lungs were too close for comfort. During these unsettling hours, the streets were quiet, and the people's defiant voices pierced the stillness of the night sky.

Whereas our home was three stories tall, my sister's home was two stories. The noise was deafening and inescapable. Cyrus nervously paced from one side of the living room to the other, while Victoria tried to console Leila.

I wondered if we were the only sane ones left. I agreed with Dad that aligning with clergy would not bring the hoped-for salvation, and I agreed with Mom that a box of horrors had been unleashed. At seventeen years old, I felt sane to not join the chorus and perhaps not sane because I had not left along with everyone else. I tried to reason with Dad, but he trusted that order would eventually be restored. He insisted that we just had to wait it out. Dad's reasoning didn't make sense to me. He should've been more cautious, especially since he had been born in the ghettoes Iran had once imposed on minorities while the Holocaust was happening in Europe. The situation in the country was serious, and like everyone else I knew, I too wanted to get out of harm's way.

*

The following Saturday morning, I went with Dad to the Yousefabad Synagogue, taking the scenic shortcut through Shafaq Park. Locals used to sit by the circular fountain and around small tables to play backgammon, but today the park was barren.

The synagogue, from the outside, looked like any other ordinary building in a residential area. Behind the nondescript metal front door was a shaded foyer, which opened onto a courtyard. During the High Holidays of Rosh Hashanah (the Jewish New Year) and Yom Kippur (the Jewish Day of Atonement) the courtyard was tented and used to accommodate the overflow crowds. Our neighborhood had one of the highest concentrations of Jewish families in Tehran, and the synagogue was one of the city's largest.

On the walls of the main sanctuary were large murals of the prophet Moses holding the Ten Commandments and of Moses's brother Aaron. These flanked the large, carved wooden doors of the ark that housed the handwritten Torah scrolls. The pulpit at the front was elevated. Services were led by prominent members of the community.

Today, a boy of thirteen was celebrating his bar mitzvah by reading the week's Torah portion and offering his commentary and insights. This rite of passage for males marks their full participation in religious observances. In addition to the *kippah* (skullcap) that all males wear, the bar mitzvah (as he is known) receives his first tallit (prayer shawl), usually white with black or blue stripes at the borders. In Iran, only boys celebrated this religious rite of passage, and unlike my female cousins in England, I didn't get the chance to celebrate when I turned thirteen. (*Bar mitzvah* means "son of the commandment," and *bat mitzvah* means "daughter of the commandment.")

The bar mitzvah's commentary echoed the primary concern of our community: Will we continue to be free? In the end, members congratulated the teen and showered him with *noghl* (sugarcoated slivers of almond). The women burst into the traditional ululation, a long, rhythmic, high-pitched sound produced by pressing (and releasing) the tongue to the palate. The custom, an expression of joy, is practiced by Mizrachi Jews who originate from the Middle East.

Each Saturday, services conclude with the recitation of the names of loved ones who died recently and in prior years at this time and with the mourners' prayer (Kaddish). Congregants wish one another a "Shabbat Shalom" (a peaceful and good Sabbath).

Every week, the prayers were the same, but fewer people attended. I noticed that Mom's hairdresser, Danny, a regular at Saturday services, was missing. Dr. Bostani, our dentist, and Mr. Rahmani, a family friend, were there alone, having sent their respective spouses and children abroad. The decline in youth attendance was most dramatic. Many of my classmates had already left Iran, and each week I noticed that even more friends were absent. How many of us will be around when the schools reopen? Each of them said he or she was going to return "when things settle down."

The synagogue served as a gathering place to share the most reliable, latest news about the community. Dad was surprised to hear that most of those who remained were considering leaving or had plans to leave despite the many challenges of emigration. One had to abandon businesses, property, homes, personal belongings, and leave friends and, often, family members. One had to arrange for sponsorship and visas and secure transportation. Not everyone had the financial means to drop everything and leave. Not everyone had relatives and friends abroad to pave the way to a new life elsewhere. Everyone did their best to cope with the extraordinary circumstances. The most difficult decision was whether to leave or to stay.

I listened to the flurry of tense, fraught comments.

"The situation is not safe. I am sending my wife and children out of the country."

"My Muslim neighbor told me that I could leave all my property to him."

"The Baha'is and the Armenians feel the same way as we do."

"I heard that in the Karaj suburb [on the outskirts of Tehran], a concentration camp is being built for the Jews."

"The Jewish community, as well as the other religious minorities, have been in this land for over two thousand years."

My father said, "The rumor of confining the Jews is malicious gossip. I'm sure it cannot be true."

"There are not enough planes for all the people who want to flee."

"The foreigners are being evacuated by their governments."

"The Shah will be forced to leave the country."

That evening, like every other, millions took to their rooftops and balconies shouting: "Allahu-akbar. Allahu-akbar. Allahu-akbar." As I drifted off to sleep, I recalled the concerns of our friends at the synagogue. For the first time, I began to wonder if Dad's optimism was tinged by denial.

CHAPTER 9

The Man in the Moon

The following week, after services at the synagogue, Dad and I walked home, saying nothing. As if for the first time, I noticed the profusion of flyers for house sales that were posted and pinned all around the neighborhood, in local shops, on tree trunks and light poles, and on the exterior walls of buildings. People were selling their belongings for next to nothing, with one goal in mind: Get out of Iran, and as quickly as possible. I could feel the earth beneath me grow shaky and unstable.

When Dad and I walked in the door, Mom greeted us with a look of despair. "Claire called. They're leaving Tehran on an El Al flight evacuating Israeli citizens. We'll go over tomorrow during the house sale and say goodbye." I had known the Besharats my whole life. Mom and Claire had been close friends for more than twenty years, and I was fond of their daughter Orly.

We continued to live our days as normally as we could, but life was anything but normal. There were long lines for essentials, such as milk, eggs, and bread. In the prerevolution era, my family would dine at the fine restaurants of Upper Pahlavi Avenue in northern Tehran, followed by coffee, tea, and pastries in the lobby of one of the high-end international hotels. Waiters in white gloves served our drinks and treats on round, silver-colored trays, while we discussed our plans for the weekend. Now, Dad would leave the house at six in the morning to stand in line to ensure that he would get his hands on our basic dietary needs.

Most of the country was on strike. Tens of thousands of workers at schools, government ministries, post offices, and other businesses and institutions took to the streets and demanded the release of political prisoners. Most crippling was the strike by anti-Shah workers at the Sherkat-e Melli-ye Naft-e Iran (National Iranian Oil Company), creating a severe fuel shortage. Ebi was quite upset as it limited his frequent trips to Tehran. We continued to speak daily by phone and share our safety concerns.

Meanwhile, Dad and I spent our days standing for hours in long lines for the rationed kerosene at the kerosene distribution center a few blocks from our home. Mom stayed indoors for fear of being targeted as an English-speaking foreigner. The kerosene was our only source of fuel for our and Victoria's heaters. In the frigid weather, Dad and I would walk home carrying the heavy plastic jugs. Dad would wrap his scarf over his fur hat to protect his face and ears from the cold wind. I would bend and stretch my stiff fingers inside my gloves.

On street corners, alongside the flyers for house sales, were notices of the locations of the next demonstration. Graffiti (most popular was "Death to the Shah") was written everywhere. Angry mobs marched through the streets. The days were cold, dark, and gloomy. In addition to fuel rations, electricity was rationed, and water shutoffs were frequent.

Victoria and Cyrus with Leila alternated their overnight visits between our house and Cyrus's parents' house. In the evening and because of the power cuts, we sat by candlelight. We huddled in one room and closed the doors to all other rooms in our spacious house. Schools remained closed, and therefore, Dad, a professor at two universities, and Victoria and I, students, had nowhere to go. (Ebi had finished medical school and was going through residency training in surgery, which was a salaried position).

During the day, when home, I liked to sit on the white marble ledge of my bedroom window. My room, situated above the garage, was elevated from the rest of the main floor of the house by a few steps. My windows spanned almost the entire north side of the house and overlooked the street. Through the open windows, I could see and hear the goings-on of our neighborhood.

That afternoon, I saw Mr. and Mrs. Hekmat leave the house. One noticeable difference between the societies of the East and the West was the way men and women walked together. Traditional Iranian culture dictated that the woman walks behind her man. I regretted the way Mr. Hekmat always walked five to seven steps ahead of his wife. Mrs. Jabari was in her front yard watering the potted plants. The same group of boys was smoking cigarettes in front of a favorite hangout, the grocery store at the corner.

When I needed solitude, all I had to do was draw the cream-bordered curtains, cutting myself off from the outside world. That particular evening, though, I felt differently. Everything was quiet, and all I could see was the dark sky of Tehran filled with twinkling stars. At that late hour and with the danger that lurked in every corner of the country, people felt safer staying indoors at home. No one was out. The moon appeared peaceful, like a bright light over a disturbed city. Suddenly, a bearded middle-aged man appeared, walking on the opposite side of our quiet residential street toward the wide intersection.

Why is a man roaming the streets at this late hour? Where is he headed? I stared at the strange scene that I just happened to see. My first impulse was to run and wake up Mom and Dad, who were fast asleep in their bedroom on the other side of the house. But I remained motionless.

Suddenly and without concern for the late hour, the stranger spoke in a loud, clear voice, "*Aks-e Imam dar mah ast.* [The Imam's image is in the moon.] Aks-e Imam dar mah ast."

What on earth was he saying? I looked up at the moon. I studied the dark spots on its round surface and strained my eyes to trace out an old, frowning man with a long beard. Well, the moon always had dark, murky spots on it. I suppose if one used his imagination, maybe it was possible to make out the face of an old man.

I shook my head, "Get a grip on yourself, Jacqueline. Stop this insanity. A maniac is wandering the street and proclaiming something ridiculous—utter nonsense—and you're listening to him?"

On the other side of the house, Mom and Dad slept through the mad chatter. I was the only one awake. I decided to keep quiet about what I had witnessed. How stupid would I sound: "Mom, Dad. Last night, a man in the street was hollering that the Imam's image was in the moon." They would laugh and reassess my intelligence. I felt embarrassed for having even looked up at the moon.

Deep in my heart, I knew he was not a lunatic wandering the streets at that time of the night. A deranged person would be kept indoors and hidden from society, and certainly would not be roaming the empty streets at that hour. Rather, he was part of the organized effort to foment discontent and rouse fury among the people.

The next morning, the city was abuzz with the news of the Imam's image appearing in the moon. Apparently, the previous evening many men blanketed the city announcing the miracle. I was not the only one to have looked up. People standing in line for bread, walking in the park, and even my taxi driver had also seen the Imam in the sky.

"I saw the Imam's face and his long beard in the moon."

"Did you take a good look at the moon last night? The Imam Khomeini's image was there."

"This is divine. Even the heavens have high regard for our leader."

"Obviously, his image is worthy of being displayed in the moon."

When Farkhondeh, our maid, walked in the house, she was beaming with pride. "Imam Khomeini is the one who will free the *mostazafin* [the downtrodden] from the tyrant. I too saw his image in the sky."

"Farkhondeh, when it's dark, the moon is over half the world. When we are under cover of night, the other side of the world is in daylight. People in other parts of the world don't care about Iran. The moon doesn't just belong to us."

"Jacqueline khanum, (Ms. Jacqueline), everyone has seen the image of the Ayatollah in the moon."

How gullible people had become to believe anything they were told. I wanted to discuss this with Sima, who happened to call that afternoon. She said it was urgent, and we planned to meet the next morning at the Vanak roundabout. Dad no longer allowed me to take public transportation, so the next day he drove me to meet Sima.

As I got out of the car, I saw a girl approach. She looked like my friend, but what was she wearing? "Sima, is that you? What on earth do you have over your head? You look ridiculous."

Sima had clumsily rolled back her plaid neck scarf over her head and had tied it under her chin. "Jacqueline, I'm scared. Where is your scarf?"

"I don't have one. Why should I wear one?"

"Haven't you heard the rumor that they are throwing acid in the faces of women who are not covered? It's too dangerous."

From the other side of the street, I caught the foul smell of burning rubber and saw black smoke and flames rising from the car tires piled up in the middle of the road. A young man standing by the tires was shouting revolutionary slogans. The mayhem had now spread to the northern district of the city, where we lived.

"Marg bar Shah. Marg bar Shah," chants calling for "Death to the Shah," went on and on.

Sima grabbed my hand. "Quick, let's get out of here. You should always carry a scarf in your bag, Jacqueline. I don't want you to be out on the streets without one. You never know when a revolutionary kind of emergency will arise. But that is not why I wanted to see you. I have something to tell you."

"What?"

"I am leaving. I am going to America in the next few days. An uncle in New York has agreed to take me in. I wish I knew English the way you do."

In the last few weeks, almost all my school friends had left the country. A Jewish organization facilitated the departure of my cousins to the United States via Austria, and now my best friend was also leaving me. I remained quiet and tried to hold back my tears.

That evening I went to Sima's house. Instead of going to sleep, we huddled in the exterior staircase between the first- and second-floor condominium units and sobbed and talked through our tears until five in the morning. Finally, Sima said, "I promise you, no matter how many years we may be separated, we will one day be reunited. I am sure of this. I will write and tell you about all the things I'll see in America."

*

The next evening, the moonlight shone on the edge of my windowsill. A few stars twinkled. The dark sky of Tehran hovered over me like a large dome. I felt emotionally drained. The phone rang. It was Ebi.

He talked about the plans he envisioned for the future. He had two-and-a-half more years to finish his residency training. After that, he had options: a respectable and financially secure life as a surgeon in Iran or, if the situation took a turn for the worse, an education and a degree that would be recognized in the United States. Either way, Ebi's future was bright, and he wanted me to share it with him.

Our romance had blossomed in a landscape of turmoil. I knew that Ebi was an exceptional person. I was too young to get married until after I had finished high school, but in our Middle Eastern society, a young bride was not unusual or out of the norm. Ebi and I were both ambitious, smart, and bilingual. He understood the West, as he had lived in Paris and traveled throughout Europe.

If I said no and the political unrest escalated, I would have the option of leaving—perhaps with Victoria and Cyrus and his family, who were all eager to emigrate. If I said yes, regardless of any escalating chaos, I was committing to at least two-and-a-half years in Iran. Neither scenario was certain.

The community was divided between the few optimists (like Dad) and the many pessimists (like Cyrus). Dad suggested that my stay in Shiraz would be temporary, and while there, I could attend Pahlavi University once everything settled down and schools reopened. My grades would be transferable anywhere. Ebi and I could eventually move.

Although acceptance to Pahlavi University was highly competitive, I would surely score high on the English portion of the entrance exam, which would increase my chance of acceptance. Shiraz was a picturesque city, and although it had caught the revolutionary fervor, I imagined that our lives together in the south of the country, closer to the neighboring Persian Gulf states and Iraq, would be quieter than in Tehran. What could possibly go wrong in two-and-a-half years?

On his next visit to Tehran, Ebi and I got engaged in a small ceremony at my parents' home, followed by a modest dinner. Our guests were Victoria and Cyrus, Ebi's sister Haleh and her husband, and a friend of Ebi's from medical school and his wife. Due to the rapidly deteriorating political situation and extreme gasoline shortage, none of Ebi's family in Isfahan was able to make the trip. Ebi had gone to drastic measures to get to Tehran, and at eighteen years old, I had just made the most significant decision of my life.

FIG. 9. Me, age eighteen, and my fiancé, Ebi, Tehran, 1979.

CHAPTER 10

The King Is Crying

On a brisk January morning, Victoria arrived with Leila unannounced, urgently pressing the doorbell. From upstairs, Mom parted the curtain and called out for me to let them in. I pressed the intercom button to unlock the front door and ran to greet them. Victoria appeared distraught, and her lips were pursed. She did not bother to look at me.

"Is Dad home?"

"Yes. What's wrong?"

"I have to talk to you all. It's important."

I offered to take the baby, but she passed right by me and climbed the stairs two at a time. What had gotten into her? What was so urgent? I hurriedly followed. She put Leila in the playpen, and Mom, Dad, and I sat across from Victoria on the burgundy leather sofa in the family room.

Victoria said, "Cyrus can't stand the situation anymore. The 'Allahu-akbar' madness on the rooftops and the riots have gotten to him. He says one day they will come inside and loot our homes. Dad, why do you remain so optimistic? Everyone who can leave is leaving."

Dad was quick to answer, "I am an intellectual, not a businessman. I will not risk leaving everything behind because I know it will all be confiscated. The Shah is still in the country, and he will put an end to all this. Besides, I'm in my late fifties. How can I start all over again?"

"Cyrus's parents don't think as you do. Well, they have three sons studying in the States. His father has already sent as much money to America as he could via the black market."

"Cyrus's father is a businessman."

"Yes, and his father believes that the situation will get worse. They are wrapping all their and our valuables, the silver and Persian rugs, and sending them by freight to family in America. We have booked tickets. We leave in a few days, on Wednesday morning."

Mom gave out a loud cry and put her right hand on her chest. "Oh my God! You are dropping everything and leaving with a suitcase? Cyrus's English is not that good. What job, prospects, and future do you have in America? Your house, his career, all your money is here. You have a baby. What about us?"

Mom was crying. Dad was quiet and remained in deep thought. Baby Leila was our pride and joy. How could we continue living without her near? I, too, had my own selfish agenda because, during those unsettling times, I needed Victoria more than ever. How would I manage to go through life without my oldest friend? How could they close the door of their beautiful home, abandon their belongings—and just leave? Where was the logic in this? The universities and the schools had been closed for the past two months, and the country was collapsing, but at least we were all together.

Victoria continued, "All of us will be staying with one of Cyrus's brothers in Los Angeles. If the situation improves, we will return."

Monday night, Victoria, Cyrus, and baby Leila visited us for the last time. It was one of the most difficult nights of our lives. We gathered at home, hugged, and said our goodbyes. Suddenly, the electricity went out. Like ghosts, we stood in the shadow of the candlelight and took one last photo together. Just like others, our family, too, was ripped apart.

*

The next day, Dad and I drove along Pahlavi Avenue to buy a large duffle bag for Victoria's hasty departure. We got stuck in a traffic jam, but it did not seem like the usual congestion. Buses and cars were at a standstill. Men, women, and children, either in vehicles or standing on the streets, could not hide their jubilant emotions. I saw a man holding up the cover page of the *Ettela'at* daily newspaper above his head with outstretched arms for everyone to see. I had never before seen such a huge font headline printed over one-third of the page in bold black ink.

Two words filled the top of the front page: "SHAH RAFT!" ("The Shah Has Left!"). Where were the many honorific titles of the king? How could the national paper dare refer to him as simply "Shah"?

In the streets, hordes of people were congratulating one another on the Shah's departure. My father rolled down his window and pretended to smile and show his excitement to blend in with the crowd. Dad always knew how to respond to the locals. A young man approached our car with a box of sweets. Dad took two pieces, one for himself and one for me. He acknowledged the moment of the people's victory with a broad smile. Next came a woman with a headscarf that covered her forehead. She placed a long-stemmed carnation under one of our windshield wipers.

Until this period of revolutionary fervor, I had rarely seen women or girls wearing thick large headscarves that covered part of their faces. Traditional women had been content with wearing the chador, but now covering heads and wearing loose clothing had become an expression of rebellion.

We managed to get home a few hours later, as the sun was setting over the horizon. Mom had heard the news on the radio and was worried by our long absence. We sat nervously in front of the television and watched a replay of the day's nightmare.

The distressed Shah, accompanied by his wife, Queen Farah, headed toward an airplane. Eighteen-year-old Crown Prince Reza had been in the United States for some time training as a fighter pilot. His Majesty looked broken, beaten down, and vulnerable. Instead of wearing his usual fancy military uniform with its many medals pinned to the jacket, he was dressed plainly in a dark suit bereft of insignia. The departing Shah did not look like royalty but instead like an average man—only shorter and thinner. Queen Farah was as elegant as ever, dressed in a long coat, high-heeled boots, and a fur hat. She looked straight ahead, and her posture was straight. Only her face revealed her confusion and distress, as she held back tears.

The inevitable day was difficult not only for the royal family but also for the Shah's retinue and other supporters. Men dressed in military uniforms and dark suits bowed to the royal couple, while others kissed the Shah's hand. The King of Kings had fallen, and just like Humpty Dumpty in Mom's nursery rhyme of my childhood, all the king's men couldn't put him together again.

According to the official announcement, the royals were flying "overseas to Egypt for a few weeks' rest." But everybody knew that this was not going to be another royal holiday. In the copy of the evening newspaper that lay on the sofa in our living room, I looked at the last photo of the Shah on the right-hand side of the front page. As he and the Queen were ascending the steps of the jet, the Shah had turned back to see his country for the last time.

The king and queen, too, must have heard the nightly cries of "Allahu-akbar" from the palace windows and seen the graffiti throughout the country. What hope did they have to remain in a place where they were no longer wanted? The Shah had finally succumbed to the people's will and left the nation that two Pahlavi monarchs, father and son, had ruled for the past fifty-four years. On that day, 2,500 years of monarchy in Iran had ended.

*

The next morning, Mehrabad Airport was packed. Foreigners, religious minorities, associates of the Shah's regime, and many others were desperate to leave, now more than ever. But not every would-be traveler had a ticket. There were not enough planes to meet the demand, and there was only one international airport in the entire country. The scene was sheer pandemonium. People were screaming hysterically and shaking their fists. We were not the only family sobbing through the last farewell. My sister and her family were among those who had confirmed seats. They were leaving behind luxurious homes and comfortable lives in Iran. They were leaving us behind.

Victoria held Leila with one hand as we struggled to shove the rest of their carry-ons into the duffle and zip it closed. Victoria carried Leila, and I lugged her Samsonite bags. Cyrus and his parents walked in front of us.

After they had boarded, I stood at the floor-to-ceiling windows of the terminal and watched the plane carrying my sister, and her family, take off. Victoria had left on short notice without much preparation and without giving me a chance to say a proper goodbye. I had already lost my closest friends, but now I had lost my closest, lifelong, confidante. Everyone was leaving for the free world, while I was left behind. I was left behind to witness anarchy. Up to this moment, Mom, Victoria, and I had been the three musketeers: inseparable. From now on, we could not be more geographically apart.

My parents were staying in Tehran. Victoria was heading to Southern California with her husband, who was unfamiliar with the language there and had no means to support his family. I was moving to the south of this vast country, to Shiraz, where its people had different customs, a unique accent, and an unfamiliar way of life. I felt like a lone tree anticipating a storm. The popular song "When Will I See You Again?" by the Three Degrees came to mind.

Mom, Dad, and I went to Victoria and Cyrus's house. We spent hours throwing out the perishables in the refrigerator, bagging the utensils and canned food to give to the maid, and wrapping up photographs and a few other keepsakes to ship. I closed the windows and emptied the garbage. Over the next few days, we packed the rest of their belongings to be sent by freight to America, which was costly. A few months later, Cyrus sold their house in Tehran and was able to keep the proceeds.

In two short days, I had witnessed the planes of the king of Persia, and of my sister and her family, take off and leave Iran. I was left behind. I felt my last glass pillar of security shatter into a million pieces, like a vale of tears.

CHAPTER II

Utopia?

I shall never forget the events of February 1, 1979. Ayatollah Khomeini returned to Iran, after fifteen years in exile. The Shah and Queen Farah had fled two weeks prior. For the past few months, the Ayatollah had led the revolution from the Paris suburb of Neauphle-le-Château. Before his asylum in France, he had spent most of the interim in Najaf, a Shia holy city in neighboring Iraq. The Ayatollah had repeated that he would return only when the Shah had left. His supporters echoed: "Only when the devil departs, the angel will arrive."

The day was one of the rare times in my life that I was afraid of what might happen to the country. The Ayatollah had openly condemned the Shah's program of Westernization, the foreigners living and working in Iran, and the countries of the United States and Israel. The condemnation of Israel was a concern for the Jewish community, which had close ties there.

During the reign of the Shah, El Al airlines had regular flights between Tel Aviv and Tehran. The Shah's government was the second Muslim-majority nation (after Turkey) to recognize Israel as a sovereign nation. Many Iranian Jews traveled to Israel for medical reasons, to conduct business, and to visit their Iranian Israeli relatives. My family had also traveled to Israel twice to visit my great-uncle and his family, who had emigrated from Isfahan in 1950. However, the majority of the Iranian Jewish community had stayed put in Iran and thrived. The Jewish community of Iran, as well as the other religious minorities, considered themselves to be proud and productive members of Iranian society and had no reason to leave their comfortable lives behind.

Since the beginning of the demonstrations, and the rapid changes that had occurred within the past seven months, Islam—the faith of the Muslim people—had been the guiding force of a new Iran. Religious minorities (such as Zoroastrians, Jews, Christians, and the Baha'is), by default, were cast aside and became outsiders. Various Iranians, Muslim and non-Muslim alike, fled the country. Tens of thousands of Jews, from a community of almost one hundred thousand, left Iran, abandoning vast amounts of property. Generally, the ones who did leave were people of means who had prospects elsewhere. HIAS, the Hebrew Immigrant Aid Society, also assisted those who wanted to emigrate.

My siblings and their families, Aunt Pouran and Uncle Darius, my cousins, and almost all of my friends, who represented many faiths, had left Iran. Mom had not worked since her return from recuperating in England. I was her youngest child, and the only one left behind to be with. My father's unwavering optimism now seemed like stark denial. My fiancé, already a doctor, was hanging on to his hope to complete his training. The residency training was five years. The first year, known as the internship year, coincided with the last and seventh year of medical school. Ebi had two-and-a-half years remaining to become a board certified general surgeon.

As my parents and I were glued to the television, which was, more than ever, our window to the world, I looked at my mother's confused face. Unlike her, I could pass. I could blend in because I was fluent in the language and had no accent. Fortunately, our neighbors and the local shopkeepers had known my mother for years and respected her. As the wife of an Iranian, Mom was looked upon as an adopted Iranian. Mostly, she did not leave the neighborhood unless accompanied by my dad or me. It was safest for Mom to stay at home. Even though being English, French, or Canadian was preferred to being American or Israeli, expats were still treated with antipathy as pampered outsiders.

During the broadcast of the Ayatollah's return, Ebi called from Shiraz, for the third time that day. He was beside himself with concern for us. Khomeini supporters in an ecstatic frenzy were near our house, and I could hear the crowds on nearby streets.

The newscaster said, "Seven million victorious people are lining the streets to the airport to witness the return of their Redeemer. The Imam has returned!"

People were laying flowers in the path of the Ayatollah's planned route from the airport to Behesht-e Zahra, the largest cemetery in Iran, and where many martyrs of the current uprising were buried. Others held banners praising the Ayatollah and posters of his photograph. Near the airport, crowds had surrounded Shahyad Monument, the tower that the Shah had dedicated on the final day of the two-and-a-half millennia anniversary festivities nine years earlier. Bursting with joy, their cries pierced the sky.

"*Khomeini, ay Emam*. [Khomeini is our Imam.]"

"*Shah raft, Emam amad*. [The Shah left, and the Imam has arrived.]"

"Allahu-akbar."

As Dad and I watched the scene replayed, I called Mom back into the family room. "Mom, come and see him on the plane." The Ayatollah was sitting by the window, looking onto the clouds. His hands were neatly folded and resting in his lap. Seated to his right was Sadegh Ghotbzadeh, a tall, slim, clean-shaven man wearing a suit, who was part of the Ayatollah's inner circle.

A foreign reporter got up and approached their seats. He knelt down in the aisle and asked, "How does the Ayatollah feel about his return to Iran?"

Ghotbzadeh turned toward the holy man beside him and eloquently translated the question. The Ayatollah turned his head but remained motionless as he uttered one word in Farsi: "*Hichi*. [Nothing.]"

I was stunned by his apathy and indifference. "Nothing? Did he just say, 'Nothing'? How can he get away with that?"

Ghotbzadeh turned toward the reporter and quickly responded, in English, "Doesn't make any comment."

The reporter, confused and persistent, asked again, "Is he happy or is he excited?"

Ghotbzadeh repeated, "Doesn't make any comment."

The euphoric crowds grew louder as the plane, after the five-and-a-half-hour flight from Paris, approached the runway and touched down at Mehrabad Airport. The plane's door flung open, and the seventy-six-year-old Ayatollah Khomeini appeared at the top of the stairs. The French pilot, immaculately dressed in a double-breasted navy and gold-cuffed uniform and brimmed hat, offered his arm to support the elderly man. The Ayatollah clutched the two corners of his long black cloak with his other hand. His son Ahmed, behind him, kept his hand on his father's right shoulder. Others followed off the jet and down the steps.

Moving slowly and cautiously, the Ayatollah appeared calm and in control. I stared into his dark, piercing eyes and at his black turban and long, white beard. He remained expressionless amid the chanting of the cheering crowd. People were everywhere—on the rooftops, in the streets, even in the trees.

"Baba joon, why is Khomeini's turban black? The other clerics have white turbans?"

"The black turban means that he is a *sayyid*, a direct descendant of the Prophet Muhammad."

On any other day, in any other universe, I would have been a teenager in my senior year of high school. I would be concerned with my studies and preparing for my entrance exams for higher education. I would be considering which universities to apply to and then, deciding which one to attend. I would be preoccupied with the latest fashions and my popularity. Instead, I sat home with no place to go and no one to see. I had been out of school, receiving no formal education, for the past four months. I held my cold hands above the kerosene heater and watched the orange-red flames. Nothing could melt the numbness that I felt inside.

A news helicopter was filming the scene from above. As the Ayatollah's motorcade approached, the crowd grew even louder and shook their fists in the air. At the cemetery, the Ayatollah spoke to his followers. Despite his advanced age, the Ayatollah seemed to be in sound mental and physical shape and delivered his speech without the aid of notes. His manner of speaking was distinct and robust. I knew his words would have a direct and significant impact on me. Ayatollah Khomeini's vision for the future Iran was to drive out every vestige of evil, in other words, everything that was associated with the past regime.

The Ayatollah articulated what his followers most wanted to hear. For emphasis, he moved his left hand up and down as he spoke.

I must tell you that Mohammad Reza Pahlavi, that evil traitor, has gone. He fled and plundered everything. He destroyed our country and filled our cemeteries. He ruined our country's economy. Even the projects he carried out in the name of progress pushed the country toward decadence. He suppressed our culture, annihilated people and destroyed all our manpower resources. We are saying this man, his government, his Majlis are all illegal. If they were to continue to stay in power, we would treat them as criminals and would try them as criminals. I shall appoint my own government. I shall slap this government in the mouth. I shall determine the government with the backing of this nation, because this nation accepts me. . . . How can anyone appointed by the Shah be legal? We are telling all of them that they are illegal and they should go. The nation does not accept Dr Bakhtiar [last prime minister of Iran under the Shah] and the army does not accept him. Only America is backing him and has ordered the army to support him. Britain has backed him too and had said that he must be supported. . . . Someone must put this man in his place. . . . You army commanders, you generals and major generals, do you not wish to be independent? . . . Abandon your foreign masters and do not fear that if you abandon them, we will come and hang you. Such rumors are spread by your enemies.[1]

The Ayatollah's promises to the nation were met with raucous shouts of "Allahu-akbar." In Iran, shouting "God is great" became the Western equivalent of handclapping, which was now frowned upon. Now the Shah was gone and the anticipated leader had emerged. The people's hopes and dreams for a better future had finally come true. Utopia had arrived.

PART 3

Adapt

1979–1980

CHAPTER 12

My First Referendum

After Ayatollah Khomeini's return on February 1, 1979, the strikes ended, and some semblance of order returned. Schools and universities reopened, and I went back to the Ettefagh school. Dad went back to teaching at the universities. Mom stayed home and ended her career in the airline business.

I was shocked to realize that I was one of only a dozen students out of my class of forty-five seniors who returned. The rest had left the country. More disturbing, of the remaining twelve, only three were Jewish. Most of the Jewish teachers were also missing, and the Jewish principal of our school had been replaced by a Muslim woman who wore the hijab. Our history books that had chronicled the saga of two-and-a-half millennia of the Persian monarchy had been tossed aside. In English studies, our British teacher was replaced by a new Iranian teacher who did not know the language as well as I did.

Our social studies teacher emphasized that religion and politics were inseparable and that religious leaders were the most suitable candidates to rule over the people. My Persian literature teacher's first assignment for our class was for us to write about the gift of the revolution and how it had enhanced our lives. I commented how wasteful the Shah and his family had been, and repeated one of the urban legends that I had heard. "When the Shah fancied watermelon, his chefs had to cut up at least ten, and choose the most appealing slice for his majesty." My comments were well received, and I got a good grade. A Muslim classmate, a longtime student at Ettefagh, stood up to read her essay. Praising the wonders of the new order, she said that Shia Islam was the most complete faith and far superior to all others. I was surprised that after receiving so many years of an outstanding education at this institution, she would make such a comment. She received a grade of A-plus.

The new regime portrayed a country transitioning smoothly to the Islamic rule of law. This was not so. Some of the Supreme Leader's supporters were now opposed to Islamic rule. During the resistance, the Ayatollah had stressed that he was not seeking power, and wanted to return to the seminary. Once in power, he changed course.

Within a few weeks of his return, Ayatollah Khomeini announced that women were barred from becoming judges. Three days later, March 7, 1979, the Ayatollah declared that women should wear the hijab in the workplace. As explained, it was best for them to refrain from revealing their hair and the curves of their bodies to men who were "*na-mahram*" (not relatives). As hijab was applied to the workplace only, women were still seen in public in varied dress. Everyone I knew was upset by the law. Ironically, the next day, March 8, was International Women's Day. Emboldened by the efficacy of recent strikes and demonstrations, some Iranian women from all spheres of life, including nurses, teachers, mothers, and students, took to the streets.

At school, a classmate said, "Jacqueline, most of us are skipping class today. We are all going to the demonstration across the street. We are all against the imposition of the hijab, and we want the authorities to hear our voices. Thousands of women and girls, as well as men, are pouring into the streets. Are you going to join us?"

I was in a predicament. From childhood, I had learned to keep a low profile within our Muslim majority society. One important piece of advice my father had given me when I had learned of SAVAK, the Shah's secret police, was to "Never get involved with the authorities in this region of the world." So, I chose my words carefully, "I wish I could join you, but, unfortunately, I don't feel well, and I can't make it. You go, and let me know how things turn out."

Less than two hours later, my friends returned to school emotionally shaken and with horrified expressions on their faces.

I asked, "Why have you returned so early?"

"We joined thousands of women blocking the roads. With our fists raised in defiance, we chanted against the headscarf. And then, we attracted mobs of religious zealots, mostly men but also women."

Another classmate said, "They called us 'whores' and said that all we wanted was our 'sexual freedom.' We quickly dispersed and ran away."

*

That evening, I spoke with Aunt Pouran, my father's only sister, about the imposition of hijab. I was concerned that I too would be forced to wear the hijab and expressed my discomfort about tying a piece of fabric under my chin and it pressing on my throat. My aunt reminded me that as religious minorities, we were to be grateful that we were allowed to live in peace. I was not to make a big deal out of it and to follow the authority. She also told me that I would get used to it.

The next day, in addition to "*Marg bar Amrika*" and "*Marg bar Esraeel*" (Death to America and Death to Israel), "*Marg bar bi-hijab*" (Death to the women who are without the hijab) was added to the chanting playlist.

*

At the end of March, a referendum on the creation of an Islamic Republic was held in the country. From now on, according to the new order, the victorious revolutionaries were free from the dominance of corrupt Western ideals. The fate of Iran would be in the hand of Iranians, not the Shah, who was known to be the puppet of America.

We were told that in the newly liberated nation, citizens as young as fifteen could freely voice their opinion for or against a new form of government in Iran. The nation was to go to the polls and answer one question: "Should the monarchy be abolished in favor of an Islamic Republic?"

The morning of the vote, I went out to run errands. Long lines had already gathered at the polling stations. Men and women stood patiently, each one clasping his or her birth certificate booklet. (The Iranian birth certificate was about five or six bound pages.) Some women also held babies, while older children played hide-and-go-seek behind their mothers.

When I got home, I turned on the television. Reporters were interviewing voters outside the polling stations.

A middle-aged man in glasses and a Persian lamb hat said, "We are now free from the dictatorship we endured under that bastard, son of a bitch, Shah." Men and teenage boys gathered around him, smiling for the camera and indulging in their few minutes of fame. The speaker then held up his arm and declared, "The freedom that has been bestowed upon us has been divined by God."

Next, the reporter interviewed a young man with black hair who was wearing jeans and a light jacket. "Hello, Sir. Will you be voting today?"

"Yes."

"What will you be voting for?"

"The Islamic Republic."

"Why?"

"Because it is the only governance that can create a just society for all the downtrodden."

Then, the footage zoomed in on two young women. "Are you voting today?"

"Yes, we are voting for the Islamic Republic, because our religion is Islam."

"What's the difference between a regular Republic and the Islamic Republic?"

"There is no tyranny in the Islamic Republic."

I heard no one, earlier in the streets or later on TV, declaring that he was opposed to the Islamic Republic. No one truly understood how this dawn of a new era was going to change their lives for the worse.

Dad called out to me, "Jacqueline joon. Go and get your birth certificate. We are going to vote!"

"Baba joon, what did you just ask me to do? Do you really want us to go and vote?"

"Yes. It is important to get our identification cards stamped. Your mother is not home; otherwise, I would ask her to join us. Most of the people, whether they like the new order or not, are voting today for the same reason. A blank identification card is not a good thing. It may imply that your ideology is not aligned with the new regime. Moreover, it will be helpful to have a stamped ID card when we use our food ration coupons."

"I thought now that the revolution has succeeded, food rationing would be over. Well, where are we assigned to go?"

"The Yousefabad Synagogue."

I had no idea that our synagogue was (or if it had ever been) a polling station. It was my first time voting. I knew that whether or not people voted, the Islamic Republic would be established. This is what people had been chanting for months, and no other option had been put forth. This was not going to be a democratic vote, and I did not want to vote. I did not want to be there in the first place.

Dad and I walked through the synagogue courtyard and entered the grand sanctuary. Our polling station was quieter than the other polling places I had passed by today.

A few soldiers in khaki uniforms and black boots were sitting around a long folding table. The beveled soles of their muddy boots left stains on the fine, handwoven Persian rugs that covered the floor. Some had what looked like long rifles or maybe machine guns resting in their laps.

An unarmed man standing in front of the table handed me a ballot but did not step aside. I could feel the heavy gazes of the seated uniformed men around me. I kept staring at the floor and was mindful of maintaining a stern expression. I saw that there was no privacy in the voting process, and my decision would be in plain view.

The referendum was written out on a banner on the table: "Should Iran have the Islamic Republic? 'Yes' or 'No'?" The ballot was perforated in the middle. Under the imperious glares of the officials, I carefully tore the ballot in two pieces. Two large boxes, each with a slot on top, were on the table. The right box had a large, printed green 'Yes' on its front face, and the left box, a large, printed red 'No.' The colors were distinguishable from far away, and anyone could see how each person voted. I folded the yes ballot and dropped it into the appropriate box. I threw out the unused portion in the bin under the table. I then handed my birth certificate booklet to the man seated at the corner of the table. He turned the pages and firmly imprinted a red stamp on the top of page three. I picked up my booklet and put it in my purse. Dad was waiting for me by the open doors at the other end of the long table. We got out of there as quickly as we could.

Later that afternoon, Mahrookh (our neighbor who was once almost hit by a stray bullet while tending her stew on the stove) came over to check my identification booklet. "So, you got a red stamp, too?"

"Mahrookh khanum, what do you mean?"

"The Jews have been assigned to their own places of worship. We have all received a red stamp, while others have a green seal."

Somehow, I knew what she was saying made sense. We, along with other religious minorities, would possibly be subjected to new discriminatory rules. It remained to be seen, and there was not much I could do about it.

The evening news showed the latest tally from the various polling stations across the country. Finally, at ten o'clock, the stern-faced anchorman made the historic announcement in his deep voice: "The people of our nation have expressed their wish. The Islamic Republic of Iran will be established at 12:00 a.m. on April 1, 1979, as favored by 98 percent of the Iranian people." Soon after, the constitution of the Shah's government, which had been written in 1906, was declared invalid, and a new constitution for an Islamic state was created. Two other features that symbolized Iran were also changed: its flag and its name. The theocratic word "Allah" replaced the emblem of the lion and the sun on the Iranian flag. Thus, the Islamic Republic of Iran came into being.

CHAPTER 13

Executions

In the newly created Islamic Republic of Iran, many ayatollahs, who were high-ranking Shia clerics, became the new celebrities of Iran. Their familiar faces on posters and banners became ubiquitous. I soon learned their names and various government posts.

Ayatollah Beheshti became the head of the country's new Sharia judicial system and was one of the main figures to rewrite the constitution for the Islamic Republic. Ayatollah Khalkhali was appointed as chief justice of the revolutionary courts. Ayatollah Taleghani was the first "Friday imam," who gave sermons at the podium on the grounds of the huge campus of the University of Tehran, the epicenter of the weekly ritual.

A different, A-list ayatollah was chosen each week to give a sermon, which mainly covered politics and domestic and international affairs. Tens of thousands of worshippers attended the weekly prayers, which were broadcast nationally the same evening. The sheer number of men, women, and children participating was alarming, and the large crowds spilled out into the side streets.

At the prayer service, the seating was gender segregated, and the women were a sea of anonymous figures covered in chadors. Courtside seats were reserved for members of the clergy and high-ranking officials. The sermon was constantly interrupted by the crowd's approval, and their chants of death to the enemies: "Marg bar Amrika" and "Marg bar Esraeel."

Seven months before, I had been wearing a miniskirt and traveling freely back and forth to England. Now, my fellow Iranians were making death threats, sometimes to England, and most women were covered up in hijab.

The success of the clergy's rule also revolutionized the Persian language. Many words and phrases were coined, and other terms had new meanings. For example, "*taaghoot*" implied that the Shah and his supporters were idolaters and not the divine authority as were the clerics. Men and women now addressed each other as "brothers" and "sisters" and viewed themselves as revolutionary compatriots.

Arabic, the language of Islamic scripture, was now preferred over the study of other foreign languages, such as English and French. Although Farsi and Arabic have a similar alphabet, and an average Iranian may be able to read and understand a few words in Arabic, the languages are distinct and have different origins.

The names of the boulevards and streets were changed either to Arabic Islamic religious names or after a martyr of the revolution. Landmarks representing the monarchy were destroyed. Shahreza Avenue, where the university and my school were located, became "Enqelab Avenue" (Revolution Avenue). The Reza Shah's mausoleum was demolished. Old establishments were eradicated and supplanted by new organizations. Komitehs (Islamic Revolution Committees) were responsible for the security of various neighborhoods. The Pasdaran (Revolutionary Guard) was a military defense organization. Soon after the revolution, many SAVAK agents, as well as generals and high-ranking officials who had served the former regime, were arrested and put on trial.

There was no longer a separation of religion and state. The clergy, distinguished by their long *abas* (robes) and turbans, served throughout the new administration. Chief Justice Ayatollah Khalkhali, who wore a white turban and black-rimmed spectacles, oversaw the tribunals of officials who had been linked to the Shah. Anyone who opposed the new order was considered to be "*mofsed-e fel-arz*," meaning one who "sows corruption on Earth." Khalkhali had developed a new judicial concept called "obvious guilt." In his court of justice, the accused was presumed guilty if his or her "crimes" were "very clear" prior to the trial. Khalkhali's court became known for speedy trials, guilty verdicts, and executions by firing squad.

Among the executed was the former prime minister Amir Abbas Hoveyda. During my childhood in Iran, I had known our prime minister as a gentleman who wore stylish suits and a flower in his lapel and held a pipe on the side of his mouth. Then, one morning, I saw a gruesome photograph of the prime minister's lifeless body on the front page of *Ettela'at*. He was strapped to a gurney and naked to the waist; a white sheet covered the rest of his body. Every evening, on television, "convicted criminals," one by one, in weak voices, confessed to their crimes of being associated with the prior regime. The next morning, photographs of the corpses were on the front page of the newspaper.

*

Because of the horrors unfolding around me, I was counting the days for the school year to end because I no longer wanted to commute to the city center. Dad drove me to school in the mornings, and I took the public bus home in the afternoon. Senior year was supposed to have been the most challenging of my education thus far, but it was turning out to be a joke. I had had a few weeks of classes in early fall, and a few months of classes in the spring.

Under the rule of the Shah, Iran and Israel had forged close alliances and business partnerships. Israeli citizens living in Tehran had their own community and a private school for their children. But now, in the Islamic Republic of Iran, "Death to Israel" chants and associating Zionism with evil were constant.

A few weeks after the return of the Supreme Leader to Iran, the Palestinian Liberation Organization's Chairman Yasser Arafat was invited to Tehran. On the news, I watched the PLO chief grin broadly when Mehdi Bazargan, Iran's first postrevolution prime minister, handed over the keys to the former (and now evacuated) Israeli embassy. The road in front of the mission was renamed "Palestine Street."

On May 9, 1979, I was scheduled to take an exam, and Mom woke up early to make me a nutritious breakfast. I had less than two months to finish school. I just wanted to be done with this place that no longer resembled the school I had known and loved since the age of seven.

Scanning my textbooks before entering the exam hall, my friend Nilofar, who, along with Yasmin had been one of my closest Jewish school friends since childhood, came up to me.

"Jacqueline, have you heard the news?"

"What news?"

"Habib Elghanian was executed today." I recalled that Dad had once worked part time for the prominent businessman and philanthropist. Elghanian was the figurehead of the Jewish community during the Shah's reign.

"How is that possible?"

"He was murdered by firing squad this morning."

"On what charges?"

"You know, the usual charges: being a 'Zionist spy' and 'sowing corruption on Earth.'"

"I am in shock. I can't believe they did this to such a great man. What does this mean for the Jewish community?"

"I don't know, but my parents are planning to leave everything behind and get out. My dad says this place is not our home anymore."

I did not know which of Nilofar's comments was more depressing—the execution of such a prominent man or losing my last friend.

When my exam was over, Dad picked me up. As he was in his usual lighthearted mood, I realized Dad did not know the tragic fate of his former boss.

"Baba joon, have you heard the news?"

"What news? There is so much going on these days."

"They killed Elghanian."

"WHAT?" Dad said as the car swerved. "What did you say? They killed Elghanian?"

"Yes. This morning."

Visibly shaken, Dad pulled over to the side of the road and tried to regain his composure. The rest of the way home, he remained quiet, but I knew that, deep down, his thoughts were the same as mine. Had a new era of the persecution of Jews and other religious minorities begun?

*

Until the murder of Elghanian, the Jewish community had adopted a facade of optimism tinged with anxiety over the new establishment. Elghanian had a brief show trial, and, in addition to being charged as "sowing corruption on Earth," he was also accused of meeting with Israeli leaders, who were known as "the most merciless enemies of God and the Palestinian people." The bogus charges against this representative of the community considerably threatened Iranian Jews' social standing and confidence. Now, the Iranian Jewish community's existence was fraught with danger.

Three days later, a delegation of six respected Jewish community leaders was assembled to request a meeting the next day with the Ayatollah at his residence in the holy city of Qom, south of Tehran. The goal was to assure the leader that Iranian Jews, as the People of the Book, were loyal and faithful citizens of their homeland and had no affiliation with the Zionist regime.

The meeting was reported in the Iranian media. That evening, Mom, Dad, and I gathered around the television. Ayatollah Khomeini was shown seated on the floor in his modest home. Members of the delegation sat cross-legged in a circle around him. After some small talk, the Ayatollah ended his remarks with his position on the status of our religious minority group. We listened intensely to each word.

"We know that the Jewish community and the Zionists are different from each other. We oppose the Zionists, and our opposition to them is because they are against all religions. The Zionists are not Jewish. They're political people who commit actions under the pretense of Judaism. The Jewish people themselves hate the Zionists. In fact, all human beings hate the Zionists."

With these words, the Supreme Leader had established that the religious tenets of Shia Islam officially defined the government's position toward the religious Jewish (and Christian) minority as the People of the Book and legitimate inhabitants of Iran. In prerevolutionary Iran, in our neighborhood of Yousefabad, Muslims, Jews, Armenians, Baha'is, and Zoroastrians lived in harmony and mutual respect. But now, the Baha'i faith was not recognized as an official religion, and its members continued to be harassed and persecuted.

Iranian Jews had been residents of this land for two-and-a-half millennia and were deeply proud of their heritage and identity. But the reassuring words of the Ayatollah did not stop the trauma over Elghanian's unjust execution for our small community, and many Jewish families continued to leave Iran by any means they could. They believed that if they stayed, their existence in Iran would be tainted by discrimination and lack of opportunity for their children.

The remaining Iranian Jews, in order to survive, tried their best to acclimate to the new government and leadership. It was of utmost importance to keep Judaism and Zionism separate. Israel was referred to as a cancerous tumor in the Middle East. In one of his speeches, the Supreme Leader declared that if every Muslim in the world threw a bucket of water toward the Zionist state, it would be destroyed by the ensuing flood. The new law clearly stated that the practice of Judaism was legal, but supporting Zionism was a crime. Contact with Israel, whether in writing or by phone, was outlawed.

Twice, on our way back to Iran from England during our summer vacations a few years before, our family had stopped in Israel, which I considered my third homeland. But now, we had to throw away the beautiful Star of David jewelry as I helped Mom break all of our Israeli music records. These incidental keepsakes were now a threat to our safety and could be construed as evidence of our loyalty to the Zionist enemy rather than our obedience to the Islamic Republic. My correspondence with my dear friend Yasmin, who had fled to Israel a few months prior, ended, as no letters could be mailed to Israel.

My future mother-in-law, Malka, always wore a large twenty-four-karat gold coin pendant. One side of the coin depicted the twelve tribes of Israel. This was considered Jewish imagery and therefore legal. The other side, though, bore a likeness of Chaim Weizmann, a politician who served as the first president of Israel. Malka's children asked her to please throw it away, but she refused. She said that she was not going to be intimidated by the extremists now in charge. Then, one sunny day, Malka buried the coin at the foot of her favorite pomegranate tree, in the backyard of their house in Isfahan.

CHAPTER 14

My Jewish Wedding in the Islamic Republic

Five months after the return of Ayatollah Khomeini and the establishment of the Islamic Republic, Ebi and I were married in a simple ceremony in Tehran. Our wedding had a distinctly Islamic flavor because it took place on the eve of Nimeh Sha'ban, one of the most auspicious days in the Shia calendar. The holiday commemorates the birth of the twelfth and last Shia Imam, Mahdi, known in Persian as Imam Zaman. His adherents await his reappearance, which will herald justice to mankind. We chose this date because the next day was an official holiday, which made it easier for our guests to travel from Isfahan and Shiraz. By this time, I had finished high school, the country had more order, and the fuel shortage was lifted.

In the past, Nimeh Sha'ban had not been celebrated with such zeal, but given the religious tide, it became an official holiday. Under Islamic jurisprudence, or Velayat-e faqih, the Supreme Leader Khomeini was the revered imam's representative until his anticipated return. The city was in a celebratory mood. The streets were decorated with lights, and the people were joyful.

The day before our marriage, I put on my mother's wedding dress from twenty-eight years before. I had always loved the dress. Its classic, knee-length, slim fit and open neckline made me feel stylish and feminine—traits deemed sinful under the new administration. Ebi and I, along with his and my parents and his sister and brother-in-law went to Rabbi Yedidia

Shofet's office to sign two marriage documents. Ebi and I, as well as a few witnesses, signed the *ketubah*, the Jewish marriage contract that is written in the ancient language of Aramaic. We also signed the civil marriage certificate. It was a booklet (like the civil birth certificate) of about ten pages, written in Arabic and Farsi. Each page had a floral border in green, yellow, and red. The beauty of the booklet soon lost its luster, as I realized its demeaning contents.

"Does the groom have other wives?"

"*Nadarad*" (does not have) was checked.

"Type of marriage?"

"*Daeem*" (permanent) was checked.

I was getting a quick education in the marriage laws. Before the revolution, during the Shah's regime, the family protection law had greatly limited polygyny and curtailed men's unilateral privileges regarding divorce and marital issues. But now, with the clergy in power, the new regime had reinstated male dominance within the institutions of marriage and family. Not only had restrictions on polygyny been removed, but also men could have as many *sighehs* (temporary marriages) as they wanted in addition to a maximum of four permanent wives. For women, the idea of polyandry was not only illegal but considered a sin.

Temporary marriage is a legal contract between a man and a woman to have an intimate relationship. The man can already be married, but the woman must have never married, divorced, or widowed. The most important aspect of a sigheh is that it grants legitimacy to any child produced from the union. The duration of the union terminates after the allocated time, which could last from half an hour to ninety-nine years.

The morning of my wedding day, Mom took me to an unfamiliar beauty salon where a female hairdresser styled my hair. (Male hairdressers were now prohibited from having clients of the opposite sex.) In the afternoon, Neda, my sister's friend from university, who was Muslim, came over to my parents' house. Neda had become, in Victoria's absence, like a sister to me. She was generous with her time and guidance. She applied my makeup, adjusted the veil over my hairdo, and helped me get dressed in my beautiful wedding gown. Neda also gave me advice about marriage and the best Persian cookbook to buy.

Notwithstanding the holiday decorations of Nimeh Sha'ban, the halcyon days of a few years ago were gone. Victoria and Cyrus's wedding, four years before, was a grand affair attended by a few hundred guests of all faiths and many nationalities. The reception was extravagant and lively. We held hands forming a circle and danced the traditional Israeli hora around the bride and groom, who were seated on chairs and lifted in the air. Men and women, fashionably dressed in evening gowns, danced together. Some snapped the fingers of both hands in a traditional Iranian manner, known as *beshkan*. This created a clicking noise, which was a demonstration of utter joy. Others swirled their hips around as they engaged in a dance. The elderly held the hands of the children and danced to the live band's renditions of top songs by Abba, the Bee Gees, and the Iranian singers Googoosh, Nooshafarin, and Sattar. At my sister's wedding, a bar in the corner served champagne, whiskey, and lots of wine.

How could I have expected my wedding to be any different? But it was different than I would have liked. Our guest list was small, primarily comprising Ebi's family from Isfahan and his close Muslim friends from Shiraz. (Ebi is the second-oldest son of six children. One sister lived in Tehran and one brother in Houston, Texas; the rest of his siblings and his parents remained in Isfahan.) On my side, my parents and a few family friends and neighbors attended. No one else was left to invite.

The brief marriage ceremony was conducted in Persian and Hebrew. Ebi and I stood under the chuppah (wedding canopy), symbolizing our new home. My parents and Ebi's immediate family surrounded us. Rabbi Shofet officiated, as he had at my parents' marriage. He praised my parents' love and devotion to each other and wished us the same. After the recitation of the seven marriage blessings (*sheva brachot*), Ebi and I then took a sip of wine from the same cup. (After the revolution, consuming alcoholic drinks, which are forbidden in Islam, became illegal, but religious minorities were permitted to consume homemade wine for ceremonial purposes.)

Our Persian Jewish wedding ceremony ended when Ebi raised his foot and stomped on an empty glass wrapped in a cloth napkin that was placed under his right foot. Our guests burst out with the words "Mazel tov" and "*Mubarak*" (congratulations, in Hebrew and Persian, respectively). The custom of breaking the glass commemorates the destruction of the

Holy Temple in Jerusalem and reminds the couple that life holds both sorrow and joy.

While still under the chuppah, Ebi took the bottle of wine and filled a glass, which he offered to Homayoon, his former roommate, and a fellow surgery resident. Homayoon, a Muslim, came forward and drank the forbidden potion. I was grateful that no revolutionary morality guards were roaming the halls. We took a few photographs, and the party ended in the early evening.

My father's white, Iranian-made Paykan car had been decorated with red and white carnations, announcing us as newlyweds. With Ebi at the wheel, we inched through the busy traffic in the city. The full moon glowed on the hot Middle Eastern summer evening. The sycamore trees lining the streets were woven with elaborate colored lights, which reminded me of the way the city used to be decorated every year in honor of the Shah's birthday. People were excited and rejoicing in the streets. The elevated mood was contagious. Drivers of passing cars rolled down their windows and cried out to us, "Mubarak!" Others honked their horns a few times, repeating a joyful "beep, beep," which is customarily done during a happy occasion. Despite the many restrictions that had been imposed on us, I felt immense joy.

The next morning, Ebi and I left the crowded city to spend a few days honeymooning in Babolsar, on the southern coast of the Caspian Sea. Upon our return to Tehran, I packed my belongings to begin a new life in Shiraz, an unfamiliar city far away from everyone I knew—except for Ebi and his friends at the wedding. Our plan was for Ebi to complete his residency training and for me to continue my education at the Shiraz University, as Pahlavi University was now known. The revolutionary days were behind us, and I did not expect much more turmoil in our lives. I was eager to begin the next chapter of my life with Ebi.

*

The flight from Tehran to Shiraz took ninety minutes. A friend of Ebi's met us at the airport, and we drove home under the Quran Gate, a historic site at the northeastern entrance of the city. I learned that two copies of the Quran were placed in an enclosure at the top of the gate to protect and bless all who pass under it. This reminded me of the similar custom of affixing a mezuzah to the doorposts of Jewish homes, a symbol of faith. Shiraz was traditionally known as the "city of wine" and for its ancient poets and many rose gardens. However, I arrived in an era when wine was illegal, and the annual art festival and nightclubs were distant memories. Liquor stores were closed down, and consuming alcohol was punishable by flogging. Meat products, such as pork, that are not halal (ritually fit for consumption), were also prohibited.

It is said that "laughter is the music of the soul," but by the time I arrived in Shiraz, a more serious tone of virtue had replaced the joyous laughter of the past. The pop music that had dominated culture in the previous regime was banned. From now on, only revolutionary music, with its marching beat and galvanizing message of camaraderie to build a new era of independence from any foreign dominance, was celebrated. Women could no longer sing solo but had to be in a chorus and accompanied by male singers. However, the famous gardens of Shiraz were still open, and the city was still home to one of the most esteemed universities in the country. I was determined to at least begin my studies there.

The first few months in Shiraz were lonely. I did not know my way around and had nowhere to go. This is how Mom must have felt when she had arrived in Tehran. At least I was fluent in the language and the Persian culture. But I still had to acclimate to the Shirazi culture, expressions, and postrevolutionary outlook that were a far cry from those of my upbringing.

Massive changes had taken place in every sphere of life, particularly concerning codes of conduct and dress. For example, men and women did not shake hands or smile at each other anymore. Most Western-style clothing was frowned upon, and the new dress code showed the degree of one's loyalty to the new regime. Sadegh Ghotbzadeh, who had accompanied the Ayatollah on his return flight to Iran, was clean-shaven and had worn a suit and tie. Now, instead of the pointed collar, men's shirts had narrow, banded collars, which made ties obsolete.

The watchword for women was "modesty." Many females of all ages began to dress conservatively. The number of women covering themselves in hijab grew exponentially. The lightweight, printed chadors worn by poorer women were replaced by solid black chadors.

Ebi's daily schedule was unpredictable, which made planning a life together difficult. As a third-year general surgery resident, he was on call every other night. He would leave our two-bedroom, rented apartment at 7:00 a.m. and return the next day around 7 p.m., exhausted from lack of sleep. After eating a small meal that I had prepared, Ebi would drop on the couch, sometimes too weary to come to bed. The next morning, the same routine would start again.

I used my ample spare time to prepare for the next round of the konkoor (national university entrance exam). I purchased a few textbooks and began an intense course of self-study. Nothing was more important to me than receiving higher education, and my aim was to get accepted into Shiraz University, the only place I could attend. I studied, got to know the city, and made new friends.

I yearned for my carefree past life. I missed my old neighborhood in Yousefabad and its familiar streets. I missed our house and my old bedroom. I missed Victoria and Raymond and my old pals now in America, England, and Israel. I longed for a letter, but international mail took about two weeks, and correspondence with Israel was verboten. Like many areas in this small city at the time, we did not have a phone. Once or twice a week, Ebi and I would drive to the center of town and join the line to make a long-distance phone call.

Islamic Republic television programming was utterly boring. It was a far cry from my youth, when we watched the dubbed Farsi versions of American and British series. But in our house, when Mom was around, we would mute the set and turn on the FM shortwave radio to a designated station to follow the program in its original language.

On camera, anchormen and anchorwomen sat far from one another and had ceased their former lighthearted on-air banter. Most of the programs were about animals in the wild and guidance from the Muslim clerics about every aspect of the path of a virtuous life. Children's programming also taught about Islam. Interviews with superstar clerics were common. Each evening, a Persian series portrayed the kings of the Iranian dynasties as aloof tyrants.

Foreign cartoons were limited to Eastern European and Japanese imports dubbed in Persian. The censored and few Western programs dubbed in Persian highlighted how America had mistreated its downtrodden. *Roots* was a popular series about one family's heritage and plight as African American slaves. Movies that portrayed the annihilation of the native Indians by the cruel and barbaric new Americans were also widely viewed. The women in these movies wore the long skirts and dresses of the era, but their uncovered hair was often obscured by a dark shadow.

Our apartment was on the second floor of a two-story house, a short walk from the Bagh-e Eram Gardens. It did not take long for me to fall in love with the magnificent gardens and the spectacular roses and other flowers spread in beds all over the facility, reminding me of Dad's garden and how he would call me his "yellow rose." My favorite section was the tall cypress trees that lined the narrow walkway along the street. Ebi told me that during the spring, the scent of orange blossoms filled the air. Whenever Ebi's schedule permitted, we would visit the mausoleums of two of the most famous medieval poets of Iran: Hafez and Sa'adi. Both had spent their lives in Shiraz, and books of their poetry can be found in most Iranian homes.

Our Jewish landlords, the Soheilis, lived on the grand first floor. The second floor was split into two modern apartments. They had designed the home with the intention of using the upstairs for their two sons, then studying in America. The revolution derailed their plans, and the sons would not be coming back to Iran. The Soheilis, a kindly couple, did everything to help me navigate my new city and often invited me downstairs to visit. Mrs. Soheili taught me how to cook elaborate local dishes, especially Shirazi cabbage rice. The house was usually full of commotion, as the Soheilis came from a large family. Mr. and Mrs. Soheili were first cousins. The marriage of first cousins is allowed, and not uncommon, in many Middle Eastern countries. There is even an old saying in Persian that the marriage of first cousins, especially those whose fathers are brothers, had been "ordained in heaven."

Ebi and I would remain in Shiraz until the completion of his residency training. In order to survive the wait until we could go on with our lives, I was determined to adapt to the rapid political and cultural changes. I reminded myself that everything is temporary. Like Dad used to say, "This, too, shall pass."

CHAPTER 15

"Death to America"

After four months in Shiraz, I planned to visit Mom and Dad back home in Tehran. We had not seen each other since my wedding, and I had so much to tell them. The plane from Shiraz was full. I placed my tote under the seat and settled in for the short flight. One of the female flight attendants caught my eye. I had never seen any woman with her style of head covering. The dark piece of fabric covered her hair, her forehead, her neck, her shoulders, and a good bit of her upper body, too. This accentuated, even exaggerated, her exposed parts. The roundness of her face seemed to pop out, and her nose looked much larger than it really was. The covering was akin to an A-line skirt for the head and neck area, between a chador and a headscarf.

The man sitting behind me asked her what I wanted to know, too. "Why are you wearing such a large, navy head covering?"

She bit her lower lip and replied, "It is mandatory, and called a '*maghnaeh*.' It is now an essential part of the Iran Air uniform."

"What if you resist?"

"Then, I'll be promptly dismissed from work."

First, the government imposed the law of hijab on working women. Now, Iran Air required more restrictive uniforms, including the maghnaeh. What was next? Will the government enforce hijab on all females? How much longer would I be able to go bareheaded, and feel the breeze on my neck and the wind in my hair?

My concerns were justified. On an evening broadcast, Abol Hassan Bani-Sadr, the first president of the Islamic Republic of Iran, was interviewed. He stated that scientific research had shown that women's hair emitted rays that drove men insane. This was hazardous to the virtues of society, and something had to be done about it.

*

I awoke to a crisp, beautiful autumn day in Tehran, and decided to venture out. Mom wanted to stay home to catch up with laundry and mail. I assured her that I would be back soon. I felt the light breeze through my hair and zipped up my anorak. I walked a little and then took a taxi to Takht-e Jamshid (Throne of King Jamshid) Avenue, now renamed "Ayatollah Taleghani" after the modern-day theologian and the first Friday Imam.

My goal was to visit the few high-end boutiques and buy a gift for Ebi. This was the first time that we had been separated since our wedding. I stood in front of a shop window trying to decide on a gift. A wallet? No, he already has one. A belt? I do not know his size. Ah, cologne. This would be a gift that both of us would enjoy. Which shall I choose? My eyes lingered on a bottle of cologne by Yves Saint Laurent.

Meanwhile, many people were coming into the area and gathered at the intersection. With raised fists, some were chanting, "Allahu-akbar," "Marg bar Amrika," (Death to America) and "*Khomeini rahbar*" (Khomeini is our leader).

What was going on? I thought the days of protests were behind us. The revolution had succeeded. What were they demanding now? The crowds grew in number and got louder. I had a few choices. I could retreat inside a store. I could walk toward the crowd. Or, I could get out of harm's way. I chose the third option and hailed an orange taxi to take me back home. I had no idea what was happening, but whatever it was, it seemed ominous.

Dad, Mom, and I watched the coverage of the demonstration on the evening news. The large, angry mob had surrounded the American embassy, and some were climbing its brick walls. Mom looked at the screen in disbelief and turned to Dad,

"Doesn't the American embassy represent a sovereign state?"

"Ideally, yes. But things here are not normal."

The news anchor explained that a group of university students, who called themselves "Students Following the Line of the Imam," had seized the embassy, which was commonly known as the "nest of espionage of the Great Satan." The footage showed American embassy employees, handcuffed and blindfolded, being dragged out of the building to a loud chorus of cheers. I was terrified to see the threatening mobs and became concerned for the captured foreigners. How many Americans had been taken? Had anyone managed to escape this madness?

The young zealots' demands were straightforward. They wanted the Shah to be turned over to them for trial. (The Shah was then in the United States, seeking medical treatment for lymphatic cancer.) They also insisted that America apologize for its crimes against the Iranian people, especially regarding the overthrow of Prime Minister Mosaddegh in 1953. Alongside the United States and Israel, cast as Great Satan and Little Satan, England was blamed as a co-conspirator and the source of all the evil that had happened to Iran in the past. During the demonstrations that had now become routine, we heard the same slogans repeated over and over again, along with the new "*Na sharghi, na gharbi, Jomhuri-e Islami*" (Neither the East nor the West, an Islamic Republic).

*

Two weeks later, I returned to Ebi in Shiraz. The news reported that a select group of the hostages—women and African American men—were awaiting release. Ayatollah Khomeini declared his solidarity with the other "oppressed minorities" in America. Khomeini justified his clemency because "Islam reserves special rights for women [and that] blacks for a long time have lived under oppression and pressure in America and may have been sent [to Iran under duress.]"

Fifty-two hostages stayed put. The Supreme Leader said that America was unable to release or protect its citizens in Iran.

*

For the previous eight months I had spent a few hours most days studying the many complex subjects covered by the konkoor. By mid-April I had finished at least six textbooks and was well prepared. While going over a chemistry quiz, I heard the radio in the background broadcast a speech by Ayatollah Khomeini. The Ayatollah believed that the country's universities were a threat and insisted that there was a need for an *enqelab-e farhangi* (cultural revolution). He added that it was crucial to implement a new system of higher education to purge the country of immoral Western values. At the time, I didn't understand what his intentions were in reconstructing the education system in Iran.

Six days later, Ebi and I were home making dinner. The radio was playing in the background. The programming was interrupted by a joyful announcer. After praising God, he reported the news of the failed mission of the Great Satan's Operation Eagle Claw to rescue the American hostages. Eight U.S. servicemen were killed when two of their rescue helicopters crashed during a sandstorm in the Iranian desert. Ebi and I looked at each other in disbelief and expressed our sorrow over this tragedy. I was too upset to continue cooking and walked toward the kitchen windows to get some fresh air. Although we lived on the second floor, I could hear commotion in the street below. I peeked out of the window and saw some of our neighbors cheering and passing out sweets in response to the news. I quickly closed the window and felt like I wanted to vomit.

Sometimes, those deemed enemies of the state and put to death were not foreigners but locals. After the April 24 failed U.S. military rescue operation, on May 8, 1980, Ms. Farrokhru Parsa, the former minister of education of the Shah's regime, who my father had once held up as a role model for me, was executed by firing squad on charges of "sowing corruption on Earth."

Also, locally, the line separating Zionism and Judaism was a constant source of confusion for some political leaders. In the summer, Ebrahim Berookhim, the thirty-year-old son of a well-known Jewish hotelier, was executed on charges of spying for the United States and Israel. When I was a child, we spent many long summer days by the pool of the Berookhim family's hotel. As an airline employee, Mom used to reserve rooms for the foreign pilots and flight attendants at the hotel. In gratitude, the owners gave Mom and our family free, unlimited access to the hotel grounds. After hearing of the execution, Mom told me how, as teenagers, Ebrahim and my brother, Raymond, who are about the same age, would swim together in the pool.

How quickly it seemed, anyone could be labeled a spy and executed. The victims were from affluent families, and much of their wealth was then confiscated. The entire Jewish community felt intimidated and believed that if they fled the country, they, too, would have to leave behind their assets, only to have them confiscated by the authorities. But staying behind also had its challenges.

That summer, I had another reason to be upset. The news on the radio crushed all my hopes for the future. The government announced that from this day forward, all universities and higher education institutions in the country were to shut down. (The closures lasted three years.) Anyone who was already enrolled had to stay home, and no new students would be admitted to any higher education institution.

How could a country shut down all higher education for an unspecified time? What was I supposed to do during this time, at the height of my intellectual curiosity? There were no decent books to read, no foreign movies to watch, no conventional television programming. In prerevolutionary days, at the British Council in Tehran, Raymond, Victoria, and I saw classic English movies, such as *Oliver Twist* and *Pride and Prejudice*, and borrowed English-language books. From the local library, we took out Farsi-language books. But now, there was no hope for an education. Fortunately, the measure would not affect Ebi's training. His residency training was considered employment and a part of the workforce. The alliance between Shiraz University and the University of Pennsylvania had been severed, and our hope that Ebi's education would be recognized in America was crushed.

I was upset that the new ruling would also affect Dad. When we next spoke by phone, Dad said that although only in his mid-fifties, it was time for him to retire. He speculated that after the colleges reopened, non-Muslim faculty would not be welcomed. One of his colleagues, who was a Baha'i and had refrained from denouncing her faith, had been fired. I did not ask for details, having been told enough. I hung up the receiver and cried.

*

The days were long, and I was bored. Mom had told me how lonely she had been when she had first arrived in Iran. With my dad studying for a master's degree and also working, she had had enough of being left alone. One day, she got dressed in a knee-length, gabardine dress, applied her favorite orange-red lipstick, and left their two-bedroom rented apartment, locking the door behind her with a large, silver key. She was confused by the commotion in the street: cars kept on honking and vendors cried out to attract customers. She couldn't even read the street signs, but she managed to get on a city bus and arrive at the British embassy. There she found a job using her shorthand and typing skills. Through the job she met English-speaking friends, got out of the house, and helped out with the finances. Mom's narrative gave me the idea to learn how to type.

The next day, I took a taxi to Moshirfatemi Street, in the heart of the business district, and got off at the corner of Karimkhan Zand Boulevard. In a shop window, an advertisement for a women-only secretarial school caught my eye. I decided to go inside and inquire. I could learn a new skill and pass my time more productively.

I climbed the narrow staircase and opened the door. About thirty women and girls sat in rows typing. Some were slow; others were fast. I signed up for typing lessons, two hours a session for three days a week. I looked forward to the classes as they gave me a reason to wake up in the morning.

The first day of class, I was surprised to see the keyboards had Persian letters, not English letters, like Mom's typewriter at home. I kept to myself and preferred not to mingle with my classmates, particularly the religious zealots in black chadors among them. I had adopted the Persian name "Jaleh," to further blend in.

Fatimah, who sat next to me, seemed particularly keen on getting to know me. One day, she asked me, "Jaleh, what are you working on today? You seem to be so involved with your homework."

"I'm working on lesson five in chapter four."

"You have such a polished accent. It's so different from our Shirazi accent. How long have you lived in Shiraz?"

"I can't believe it, but it's been almost a year."

"Listen, Jaleh. You know that I like you, and we have been classmates for some time now. I need to ask for your home address. It's for a good cause. I have told my family so much about you, that you are so sweet and poised. They even like that you are from Tehran, although they would want to know about your family. My parents and I, along with my uncle and his wife, would like to come over and ask your parents for your hand in marriage to my older brother."

I did not know how to respond to such a request. This surely was a surprise. The scene would make interesting conversation for my family and in-laws. As humorous as I found it to be, I knew that I had to get out of the situation as tactfully as possible.

"Fatimah joon, I had no idea you thought I'm so special."

"My brother Ali is a *pasdar* [a soldier with the Revolutionary Guard]. My other brother, Abbas, was martyred during the revolution."

"I'm honored you have chosen me to be associated with a pasdar and the family of a martyr. What more can a girl wish for other than to become the wife of a guardian of our glorious revolution and its divine principles?"

"I would love for you to be my sister-in-law."

"Fatimah joon. As much as I'm humbled by your gesture, I'm afraid it is too late."

"What do you mean?"

"I'm already married. That is why I am living in Shiraz. My husband has brought me here."

"But you are so young, and you don't have a ring on your finger."

"That's because I'm pregnant. I know I'm not really showing yet. My ring doesn't fit my finger anymore because my fingers are swollen."

Fatimah pursed her lips into a pout and turned to her typewriter in obvious disappointment. I knew that I could not have conjured up a better excuse than the truth.

CHAPTER 16

Invasion

Ebi and I were looking forward to our dear friend Farhad Ghaemi's visit in August. It had been five months since he left Shiraz for a lucrative medical position in Tehran. He would arrive Thursday night and stay with us for the weekend. Farhad, a physician, had completed part of his residency training with Ebi in Shiraz. Farhad's wife, Mina, was a nurse and had helped me acclimate to Shiraz. We used to host dinners at each other's homes, and Farhad would always supply the wine from his well-stocked liquor cabinet (from before the revolution).

I was taken back when I opened the door. Everything about Farhad had changed: his appearance, his demeanor, his body language, even his choice of words. Standing before me was a bearded man with slicked back hair and a stern expression on his face. He averted my gaze and stared at the floor because I had not covered my hair.

After dinner, I suggested that the following day we drive to the outskirts of the city for sightseeing.

"It's the holy month of Ramadan. I will be fasting, and I have other plans."

"Oh." (Wow, I thought. Since when did Farhad fast?)

While putting away the dishes in the kitchen, Ebi whispered in my ear, "We need to feed him before he starts a new day of fasting tomorrow."

"Do you mean he will get up predawn to eat at four o'clock?"

"Yes."

"If your friend is now observant, then that is his prerogative, but I'm not getting up to prepare a meal for him. We are not fasting and not obligated to get up. If you want, you can get up that early. I am pregnant, and I need my rest. He is our guest, and I'll put some nonperishables on the kitchen table tonight. Let's show him what is in the fridge, so he can help himself and prepare a meal in the morning."

The next morning, Farhad left the house before we woke up. To my surprise, he had not touched anything in the kitchen. His only source of food for the long, hot summer day of fasting was our dinner the night before.

That afternoon, Farhad rang our doorbell. He looked tired and hungry, but seemed content and energized. I could not offer him anything, not even water, until sundown, when he could break his fast.

Ebi was excited to see him. "Farhad, you left so early today. Where have you been, my friend? You should have waited for me to join you."

"Today is the last Friday of the holy month of Ramadan, and as Imam has proclaimed, it is also International Quds Day."

"Yes. I do remember that last year Ayatollah Khomeini declared this day as a day of solidarity with the Palestinians and against the existence of Israel."

"I participated in the Quds Day rallies today. By the way, you should correctly refer to the country as the 'Zionist regime'!"

I remained quiet and looked at Ebi. I wanted to know why our friend, an educated physician, who, like me, was a Tehran native, had changed so much. I thought of the irony that both the Iranians and the Israelis, as the citizens of a Shia country and a Jewish State, are minorities in the Sunni-dominant Middle East. Iranians are not Arabs, but the descendants of a Zoroastrian Persian ancestry. Zoroastrianism is one of the world's oldest religions and was founded in Iran a few thousand years ago. The Arab conquest of Persia in the seventh century led to the eventual decline of Zoroastrianism in Iran.

That evening, Farhad, Ebi, and I watched the regime's propaganda programming of the footage of the tens of thousands of demonstrators in Tehran and in hundreds of cities throughout Iran. The protesters carried placards with the slogans of "Death to Israel" and "Death to America" and chanted against their two most vicious enemies. An Israeli flag was burned during one of the rallies, while the onlookers celebrated.

As the political climate of the new regime dictated and because I was a member of a religious minority, it was best to keep my thoughts to myself. Authority ruled, but not everyone was brainwashed into thinking that Zionism and the West were the twin sources of all evil. The many educated and open-minded Iranians relied on Radio Israel and the BBC's Persian radio programming from Jerusalem and London, respectively, for uncensored news.

*

The hot summer days of Shiraz continued, and my growing belly limited my mobility. I was anxious to be done with the pregnancy and reclaim my former body. As my due date, September 21, approached, my anxiety heightened. My biggest wish was for my delivery to go well and without any complications. In mid-September, Ebi and I picked up Mom, who had come to help me with the birth of our first child, from Shiraz Airport. Dad would join her after the baby's birth, and then, they would return to Tehran together.

I woke up the morning of September 20 with some discomfort. The day was significant also as the thirty-second anniversary of when my parents met, and the second anniversary of my return from London to Tehran. I had had a fitful night, tossing and turning.

By early afternoon, the labor pains began, and I became more uncomfortable as the day progressed. It was too soon to go to the hospital, but not a good idea to stay too long in our apartment. Dr. Ali Afkhami, a dear friend and a colleague of Ebi, made a surprise visit later in the day. He said, "Ebi told me about your discomfort. This will make you feel stronger." Ali held out a large tray of the most delectable golden dates from his family's private gardens in Jahrom, a city about a two-hour drive from Shiraz. I enjoyed the most delicious date I had ever had. I felt fortunate that we were surrounded by such caring friends.

In the evening, Mom, Ebi, and I drove to nearby Namazi Hospital. Ebi parked the car, while Mom helped me as I clumsily walked inside. Two nurses got me ready and strapped a fetal heart monitor to my stomach. I felt cold and asked Mom to help me put on my favorite, thick, yellow-and-orange argyle socks.

My labor pains intensified and became unbearable. I had never experienced such intense pain. My American-educated and a somewhat arrogant doctor would arrive once my labor had sufficiently progressed. Ebi spent most of the evening coming in and out of the labor room to check on me and consult in the hallway with his colleagues. Mom did not leave my side. I was also fortunate to have my friend Katayoon there. She was finishing her second year of residency training in gynecology and obstetrics. The incredible pain lasted another five hours. I practiced the Lamaze breathing technique, which I had taught myself from a book. I could not get comfortable and occasionally let out a piercing shriek.

The early hour of the next day came, and my distress grew. The attending nurse stroked my face. Then, Katayoon jumped from her seat and said that it was time to take me to the delivery room. As Shiraz was a small city and easy to navigate, the doctor was notified when it was necessary for him to be there. He had arrived at the hospital and came to my bedside.

Our daughter was born at 1:05 a.m., on September 21, 1980, in the city of Shiraz, the Islamic Republic of Iran. She had a feisty cry. She was handed to me wrapped in a cozy striped blanket, and my emotions took over. I looked at her beautiful face as her delicate hands popped out of the blanket. Then, the baby was taken to the nursery, and I was rolled into a different room to rest. Cold and shivering, I was barely covered by the thin blanket. I pulled the blanket toward my shoulders and tried not to shake too much. I was excited and exhausted at the same time. But most important, I was relieved that the delivery was safe, and my baby was healthy. With a smile on my face and immense pride in my heart, I closed my eyes and drifted off to sleep.

That afternoon, Ebi and Mom came back to see us at the hospital. We chatted and fussed over the baby and had a lighthearted conversation. I was scheduled to stay at the hospital for one more night. Ebi and Mom left, promising to return the next day. I felt blessed. I now had a family of my own and lived a peaceful life in a tranquil city. I stayed up to write a few letters. Finally, feeling weak and tired, I went to bed in the early hours of the next day, September 22, determined to get as much rest as I could.

I woke up feeling wet and cold. According to the clock on the wall, I had slept over eleven hours. The door opened, and an assistant nurse walked in to see how I was doing. She looked upset. She pulled back the blanket and gasped in horror. I was soaking in a pool of blood all the way to my knees.

"Poor thing! No one came to check on you? Someone needed to have come and changed the mat under you. Well, I can't blame anyone. At least, you were asleep and have been spared the agony of what has been going on. Get up, and go and take a shower."

"Where is my husband? Where is my mother?"

"Oh. Your mom is the foreign woman. They will not be coming tonight."

"What do you mean?"

"Go and take a shower. Now get up. Things are not normal here."

After a shower, I got dressed and wrapped a robe around me. I walked down the long hall to the nursery on the other side, to be reunited with my baby. To my surprise, the lights in the hallway and as far as I could see in the other parts of the hospital were dim and turned down to the minimum necessary. How strange. Don't hospitals need to be lit up at all hours of the night? I held onto the railing as I walked toward a large waiting room and nurses' station, where other women, who had also recently given birth, and doctors and nurses, gathered.

My eyes grew accustomed to the dim light, and I saw a nurse go to the windows to ensure the curtains were drawn shut. I noticed the worried looks on everyone's faces. One woman, who had had a C-section, had an intravenous drip attached to a vein in her left hand. She was clearly in pain following the surgery and delivery. A few of the mothers were crying. Two patients were slowly pacing up and down the corridor.

The radio was playing marching band tunes as the announcer spoke and interrupted the music: "Attention, attention! We are under attack! The Iraqis have invaded our country via air and land. The war has begun!"

I had to sit down. I had gone to sleep grateful for my family and an undisturbed life, and awoke to our country at war. I wanted to know everything about the situation.

The announcer continued, "Respected citizens! The Iraqis have conducted a surprise attack on Iran's air bases in nine cities. They have also attacked our southern borders with a massive invasion along the country's southwestern border. The enemy troops have crossed over the Arvand Rud into the Khuzestan province."

This river (known as "Arvand Rud" in Persian, and "Shatt al-Arab" in Arabic) is a boundary between the two countries. As far back as I could remember, Iran and Iraq had had a territorial dispute over the waterway. Ayatollah Khomeini had revealed his intention to export his brand of Islam and Iranian revolutionary principles to other countries in the region. Also, in light of the new government of Iran and its execution of many of the Shah's military generals, Iraqi president Saddam Hussein took advantage of the opportunity to attack Iran and capture its oil fields.

One of the hospital staff gasped, "The land attack is not that far from where we are!"

A patient cried out, "Dear Imam Hussein! Help us."

A passing nurse instructed us to keep all the curtains drawn. "No speck of light can escape the room. The Iraqi warplanes could be above us."

I recalled Uncle Philip's stories of life during the London Blitz. At the time, the stories had seemed so foreign and distant compared to my then pampered life in Tehran. I never thought that one day I would be in a similar situation. Suddenly, I wanted nothing more than to see my newborn. I got up and found my way to the nursery. A nurse helped me return to my room with the baby. I missed Ebi and Mom, who, along with everyone else in the city, had stayed in their homes after dark. I was a new mother, in the Islamic Republic of Iran, which was now engaged in a bloody war.

CHAPTER 17

The Sacred Defense

Local coverage of the Iran-Iraq War was constant. We were barraged 24-7 with news footage of buildings flattened to rubble and dead bodies scattered about and covered in dust. Tens of thousands of people had already been displaced. Refugees from the Iranian province of Khuzestan, which shared its western border with Iraq and was along the right bank of the Arvand Rud, had fled to Shiraz. Khorramshahr (meaning "verdant city"), the main city of Khuzestan, had been captured by the Iraqis. The effort to retake the city was the focus of the early days of the war and became known as the "Battle of Khorramshahr." In commemoration of the carnage, the Iranians renamed the city "Khuninshahr" (city of blood). The reach of the war was spreading to the interior of the country. The urban areas of Isfahan and Tehran were targeted, but due to the proximity of Shiraz to the border, we were at considerable risk. This war was not going to be ending soon.

At sundown, our homes, too, fell into darkness and gloom. Ebi and I used a small candle as our sole source of light. By radio, we were introduced to the air-raid siren. The screeching sound warned citizens that bombing was imminent, and to take shelter.

All media publicized safety tips, including how to apply duct tape—diagonally in the shape of a large X—to our windows to minimize glass shattering. My first evening home from the hospital, Mom, Ebi, and I, with our newborn in my arms, sat under the cold staircase of the house. Our neighbors had not yet joined us.

Ebi gave me some words of comfort, "We will get out of this mess. I will find a way to get us out of here."

We decided to name our daughter "Leora," derived from the Hebrew word "*ora*," meaning "light." However, I soon learned that, due to the regime's desire to purge the country of Western influence, the Iranian *sabt-e ahvaal* (registrar's office) maintained a list of acceptable Arabic and Persian names to choose from. Non-Muslims, however, were exempt from this imposed restriction, and we were able to name our child as we wished.

Needless to say, Dad never joined us in Shiraz. A few weeks later, Mom left with two of our friends who were driving to Tehran. My mother-in-law, Malka, took a bus from Isfahan to Shiraz to visit us. Malka, like Mom, was a source of great comfort and help.

The revolutionary fervor had taken on a renewed urgency with the Iran-Iraq War, known as the "Sacred Defense." Patriotic Iranians volunteered to defend the country against the aggressors. Ayatollah Khomeini declared that Iran would not cease fighting until Saddam Hussein's regime toppled. It was every Iranian's sacred duty to participate in the country's defense and to push the Iraqi forces back across the borders. Hundreds of thousands of young and old men from far-away towns and metropolitan cities were either drafted or volunteered to go to war. In noncombat roles, women, too, participated in the war effort.

Propaganda encouraged martyrdom as a virtue and a path. A popular slogan was "*Tanha rahe saadat, shahadat ast*" (The only way to salvation is martyrdom). Murals of war martyrs were painted on every street corner. Streets were renamed after martyrs. Photo flyers of the latest martyr were posted in shop windows. Families of martyrs received preferential treatment in all aspects of daily life. Many songs used the metaphor that beautiful red tulips were grown from the blood of the martyrs.

The volunteer paramilitary organization, the Basij, founded in April 1980, was made up mainly of young men, and they enthusiastically embraced Khomeini's call for martyrdom. Our nightly television programming showed scenes of soldiers getting prepared for war. They wore green headbands around their temples, printed with the word "Hussein," referring to the third Shia Imam, who had been martyred in the Battle of Karbala in the seventh century. These young soldiers were told that they would go straight to heaven through the path of martyrdom. They were given a key that would facilitate their entrance to paradise.

Only nine years before, Iran had celebrated 2,500 years of monarchy. I had watched the elaborate procession of soldiers dressed in historical costumes and wearing fake beards. Now, I was watching young soldiers dressed in camouflage and khaki uniforms with green headbands and holding rifles. How could the volunteers be so eager to go in the minefields and blow themselves up?

Martyrdom was praised in verse on the radio. Songs co-opted simple sentences from first-grade primers. *"Baba ab dad"* and *"Baba naan dad"* (Dad gave me water and Dad gave me bread) became *"Baba khun dad"* and *"Baba juon dad"* (Dad gave his blood and Dad gave his life). War movies and battle songs became popular.

Jumbo jets carrying a few hundred wounded militia at a time landed in Shiraz daily. Ebi spent long hours at the hospital. There were not enough beds, and the corridors were used as makeshift areas to tend to the injured. I heard gruesome stories, such as men with chopped-off limbs bleeding to death.

Since the start of the war, the country's borders had been temporarily closed. There was no way for us to leave the country. We were trapped. To evade the mandatory military draft, many families who did not want their sons to fight in the war sent their young sons out of the country illegally. They paid hefty sums to human smugglers, who drove the escapees through the desert and facilitated their crossing over the border. The journey was risky, and some never made it to the other side.

*

In the meantime, Ebi completed his fifth and last year of residency training and took the required board exams to practice as a general surgeon. He was offered a position at Shiraz University. Ebi's new status entitled us to live in the private, exclusive area behind Namazi Hospital reserved for its physicians and their families. The enclave was a quiet, lush retreat away from the commotion of the city. The residential area had twenty-two villas and three newly built apartment buildings. Our spacious and modern apartment was on the top floor of a two-story, four-unit building. From our living room window, I could watch the gardeners tend the bushes and shrubbery.

We were the only non-Muslim family living there. All of our friends and Ebi's acquaintances, who became our close confidants and trusted friends, were Muslim. Dr. Kazeroini and his wife, Zahra, were our first-floor neighbors. Zahra had grown up in Shiraz, and often reminisced about the "good old days before the revolution." Dr. Farmayesh and his wife, Forouzandeh, who were both from Isfahan, lived across the hall. They were devout Muslims. He had a short beard, and she always wore a chador. Although university educated, Forouzandeh would ask for her husband's permission to leave their house—except to visit me at my apartment a few feet away.

I had grown close to both women, but the two couples were merely cordial to one another and obviously did not like each other. Their levels of observance did not matter to me. Our other neighbors, also on the first floor, were Dr. Sadeghi and his wife, Tayebeh, who fell somewhere in between the other neighbors in religious observance. We were all about the same age and had young children.

I spent a lot of time with the women in our neighborhood, and their friendship enriched my life during the extraordinary times of the new government and engagement in a brutal war. They were valuable resources, helping me navigate daily life in my adopted city. Peymaneh taught me how to decorate my house. Sahar showed me how to do banking chores. Then there was Maryam, the wife of the only plastic surgeon in the city. He was booked nine months in advance. Taraneh's husband, a Pakistani doctor, was a serious man with broad shoulders and a thick mustache. We also made new friends among Ebi's colleagues living in other areas of the city, and we would often go to each other's homes for dinner.

We took advantage of Shiraz's mild climate and joined a group of our friends and their children to picnic at Persepolis, in the outskirts of the city. It took us just over half an hour to drive the thirty-seven miles from Shiraz to the ancient site. Persepolis, known as Takht-e-Jamshid in Persian, was the ceremonial capital of the Achaemenid kings, whose founder was Cyrus the Great. The city's treasures had been looted and its buildings deliberately destroyed by Alexander the Great, to avenge the destruction of the Greek Temples and cities by the Persians. For me, this was a special place to be, because it was the site where the Shah had had the 2,500-year ceremonies in 1971.

*

On a crisp January day, pushing Leora in the stroller, I walked to the nearby shops. Standing in line for bread in front of the bakery, I heard the crowd discussing the latest news. The night before, the television had shown footage of the released American hostages ascending the steps of the plane that was taking them to freedom. They had been in captivity for 444 days. One woman hollered, "Get lost to all of them! Good riddance! Those bastard Americans!"

I remained quiet, knowing it was best not to express my opinion, which was a far cry from that of the people around me, but in my thoughts, I wished the Americans farewell. They would land on the other side of the world to jubilant crowds. They were finally leaving, just like my sister, my cousins, and many of my friends before them. I was again left behind, but now I had a baby in tow, and my country was at war.

We went on with our daily lives, and although the aerial bombings still occurred from time to time, I was grateful that we were away from the frontlines of the ongoing battle.

A few months later, Ebi came home from work and looked distressed. I asked, "What is wrong?"

"Please sit down. I need to talk to you about something important. Promise me that you will be strong."

I sat down, bracing myself for bad news.

"Listen, Jacqueline. New orders have come that surgeons are to provide their services at the hospitals closest to the war front for one month." He hesitated for a few seconds, and then continued, "I will be taking care of casualties before they can be safely transported to more permanent hospital facilities in larger cities. I will be going by minivan from Shiraz to a city near the war zone. I will be going with two residents and a few male nurses."

"Oh, my God! When?"

"Within the next few days."

"But don't you provide valuable services here? They bring so many of the wounded to Shiraz."

"They need surgeons at the closer areas to the frontlines. I have no clue where I will be going."

"This is too dangerous!"

"I wish I could get out of it, but I can't. I want you and the baby to go to Tehran for the month that I'm away. There is no point in you staying in Shiraz. Tehran will be safer, and you and Leora will be with your parents."

I took a deep breath. I worried about Ebi's long journey in the stifling heat of the southwest part of the country. What would he eat? Where would he sleep? But these thoughts were trivial because the possibility that my husband would not make it home was more than I could bear. I looked into Ebi's face and said, "It will be one month. Then it will be over."

"There is one more thing I haven't told you yet."

"What?" (What could be worse than my husband being in the war zone?)

"I have to go one month every year. This will be the first year."

PART 4

Veil

1981–1985

CHAPTER 18

"Sister, Guard Your Hijab"

On a late June morning in Tehran, Mom, Dad, and I sat around the kitchen table enjoying a breakfast of fresh, hot *barbari* (a thick flatbread), feta cheese, cherry jam, hard-boiled eggs, and hot tea. Dad had gotten up early to walk to the bakery for the bread. Other staples, such as rice and cooking oil, were rationed and only available in the allocated amount per family. Butter had completely disappeared from the market, but other scarce food items could be found at high prices on the black market.

Dad had placed the portable short-wave radio on the corner of the long Formica kitchen table. The radio was his constant companion. Stations included the state-run programming broadcast in Iran and the foreign news programming broadcast from overseas, such as the BBC and Radio Israel (both in Farsi). As we were chatting and eating, the mundane Iranian radio program was interrupted by breaking news. Dad, sitting across from me, held his white feta cheese sandwich in midair.

The announcer said, "Attention, attention! This morning [June 28, 1981], a powerful bomb went off at the headquarters of the Islamic Republic Party. In a courageous manner, Chief Justice Ayatollah Mohammad Beheshti; four cabinet ministers of health, transport, telecommunications, and energy; twenty-seven members of the Majlis (Iranian parliament); and forty-one other leading officials were martyred today while holding a meeting at the city center.[1] This cowardly act was perpetrated by the enemies of our sacred principles."

Dad had an amused expression on his face, which made me laugh. Mom looked confused. The regime's greater use of Arabic further restricted her understanding.

"What is going on? What bomb? Where?"

I said, "Sh! Sh! Let me listen. I'll tell you in a minute."

The announcer continued, "Seventy-three holy martyrs have ascended to their heavenly abode. This tragic event is a great loss for our revolution. Attention! Attention! Today, we will mourn this great loss. Ayatollah Beheshti was not just a man, but, as quoted by Imam Khomeini, 'he was a nation.' Our enemies have underestimated the solidarity of our country. Such cowardly acts, perpetrated by our enemies, will not slow the momentum of the revolution." The announcement was followed by revolutionary music and solemn songs.

I could not believe what I was hearing. This attack by the opposition was rare and brazen and successful. Although the loss of life was unfortunate news, we did not agree with the regime's harsh laws nor share its ideology or hatred for the West. We liked the West. I loved America. I hated the imposition of the hijab. Certainly, others besides us were also astonished by the news of the opposition's surprise attack.

The most prominent resistance organization was the Mojahedin-e-Khalq (MEK). It was apparent that they were responsible for the day's attack at the party headquarters. With the success of the revolution, the authorities had begun a policy of cracking down on all opposition groups. The new regime clearly stated that it was the government of the Islamic Republic, and there was no place for any opposition.

Hundreds of former supporters of the Shah and members of opposition groups to the new regime had already been executed. We had heard the rumors and horrific stories about women and girls being raped before their executions at the notorious Evin Prison in Tehran. These heinous acts were said to be justified by the belief that virgins are guaranteed a place in heaven, and this act would preclude the accused prisoners from entering the preferred eternal home.

The evening news preempted all regular broadcasting, and we watched the speech of the Supreme Leader, who was seated on an elevated plat-form in front of a large crowd. I could never tell how the imam actually felt because his facial expression always remained the same. He began his speech with the words: "I would like to express to the clerical community, and the Iranian people, and to all Muslims and the oppressed people of the world both my congratulations and my condolences. . . . This recent criminal act has been perpetuated by America who used the traitors to commit such a crime upon the Muslims."

The Supreme Leader's words were interrupted by the weeping of men who sat cross-legged on the Persian rugs that covered the floor.

*

The next day, the mood in the country remained somber. I left the baby with Mom and Dad and headed to the many bookstores along Enqelab-e Islami Avenue (Islamic Revolution Avenue), formerly known as "Shahreza Avenue," near the University of Tehran and my old school. Once in a while, I could find a book that was either in English or in Persian about a subject that interested me.

After the revolution, the reversal of street signs from names of the royals or foreign dignitaries to revolutionary or martyrs' titles had become a new strategy to influence the psyche of the people. The new street names in the public arena reaffirmed the principles of the new order. Therefore, to the taxi driver, I had to be careful to name the streets correctly, as any mention of a former name might imply that I was pro-Shah.

My driver skillfully maneuvered through the maze of honking cars, overloaded minivans, and cyclists. Driving in Tehran was not for the faint of heart.

The first few months after my arrival in Shiraz, I took driving lessons but soon found out that driving in Shiraz would also require bravery. Pedestrians walked into traffic at will, and many of the women seemed more intent on holding their chadors over their foreheads than looking both ways before crossing the street. Entering Setad Circle, whoever had the most guts would push through the hodgepodge of cars and get ahead in no particular order. I had tried to avoid the taxis, but then would find myself driving behind a city bus at a snail's pace while black exhaust fumes filled the air. I had to roll up the car window in the smoldering heat. In both Shiraz and Tehran, the distance between cars on the road was sometimes mere inches.

I looked out of the taxi window onto the busy streets of my cosmopolitan hometown. More women were veiled than had been when I left for Shiraz. "Sister, guard your hijab" (*Khahar, hijabat ra re'ayat kon*) had become a commonplace slogan in the media and in wall graffiti. The theory was that men who were *na-mahram* (not close relatives) would always be looking at women, and the hijab would protect the female wearer from their lustful gaze. In this way, the hijab would result in a moral society. The implication was that every woman is responsible for her own safety; another implication was that hijab is an act of defiance against Western values.

On the radio, a reporter would interview women in the street and ask why they were wearing hijab. The answer was always that, by wearing hijab, they are "slapping their fist in the mouth of America." This is the same expression that Khomeini used in his speech at the Behesht-e Zahra cemetery when he arrived in Tehran.

I stepped out of the taxi and walked along the south side of the street. A young girl in a headscarf offered me a leaflet. She looked nervously side-to-side while holding tight to her bag, which apparently held the rest of the flyers. I knew whatever she was handing out was not sanctioned by the administration, and this meant danger and trouble. I recalled Dad's oft-repeated credo that I should not get involved with or challenge authority in this part of the world. The girl shoved the leaflet into my chest as if pleading for me to be quick. I was not interested in anyone's propaganda. My only interest was in staying out of trouble. I knew that if I continued to be a law-abiding citizen, whatever the law, I would be safe. I shook my head no and sped up to pass by her.

I browsed the bookstores but found nothing of interest. I continued to Farah Park and entered its gates. The park had been renamed "Laleh Park" after the tulip, a symbol of martyrdom. When I was a child, tulips were my favorite spring flower in Dad's garden, and Farah Park had been a favorite destination with friends and, later, with Ebi during our courtship.

I wanted to recapture a bit of my past there, to stroll on the tree-lined paths and reflect on my life as a new mother whose husband was serving the country as a medic near the frontlines. Deep in thought, I noticed someone trying to speak with me. I stopped and saw a young woman veiled in a black chador and a man at her side. He stayed in the background as she approached. "Excuse me, Sister. May I please ask you to open the zipper of your tote bag and show me the contents?"

I had many confused thoughts in the next few seconds. What an odd request. Who did this woman think she was to demand to see the contents of my bag? I recalled Sima's remarks the last time we met before her hasty departure: "Jacqueline, always have a scarf in your bag. You never know when you may encounter a revolutionary emergency."

All working women had to conform to the Islamic dress code in the workplace, but because of women's initial resistance, the regime had not tried to enforce the code of hijab on all women. Some women in the streets dressed as they had in the prerevolution era—in slacks, shirts, and jackets, albeit more modestly.

Women, in general, still had the option to cover or not cover their hair. I chose the latter and wore my hair in a ponytail but felt extremely self-conscious when in public. I had heard rumors about the dangers of not covering your hair. I had also heard that the authorities created morality patrol units to roam the city streets and neighborhoods and enforce women of all religious groups to follow the Islamic dress rules in public. This meant that all women and girls had to cover their heads with a scarf and their bodies with loose clothing, only exposing their faces and their hands up to the wrist. Anyone who opposed the morality police could be reprimanded, detained, or taken away. Who knew where the resisters were taken and how they were treated? Were they fined? Jailed?

The morality police pair who stopped me seemed different. I was impressed by the woman's politeness. I had nothing to hide, relieved that I had refused the leaflet the nervous girl tried to hand me earlier. I confidently held my head up and said, "Of course, you can see inside my bag." I opened the zipper of my tote and handed it to her.

She rummaged through its contents, including my house keys, my wallet,

FIG 10. At age eighteen, before the enforcement of hijab, 1979.

FIG 11. At age twenty-one, after the enforcement of hijab, 1982.

and my shopping list. Suddenly, her hand emerged from the depths of my bag, holding a light cream chiffon headscarf. "You bloody whore! You carry a veil in your sack, but don't wear it?"

How dare she talk to me in such manner. I got defensive and said, "At least I have one with me!"

"You *gharbzadeh* [someone who is enamored with the West]. You deserve to be treated as a sex object for men, as the women in the West are. How dare you carry a headscarf and not wear it. It is women like you who cause social corruption on the streets of our city."

I froze in disbelief, unprepared for the insults. I realized I had made a mistake by confronting authority. Not everyone in the park was wearing a headscarf, so why was she picking on me? I pressed my lips together, ready to give her a mouthful of what I thought about her. I noticed the man behind her move his fingers over something tucked under his jacket. Think, Jacqueline, think! What would Dad do? He always knew how to keep the peace. I needed to apply his diplomacy to tame this wild beast who had power over me.

"Sister, what you are telling me is correct. I do apologize. A decent woman refrains from showcasing the curves of her body to strange men. My clothing is modest, but as you can see for yourself, the headscarf is a chiffon fabric. I have learned my lesson that this material is not suitable for covering my hair. It is slippery and keeps rolling back. I will need to sew myself a *maghnaeh* [a head to shoulder upper body covering] in thick cotton so that it will stay put and sufficiently cover all the strands of my hair. I do apologize."

Her facial expressions softened. My appeasement had worked. She turned around and glanced at the man, and then back at me. "Okay. So, use a cotton scarf."

"Yes, I will. I know how to sew, and I will sew my maghnaeh today."

Without saying another word, they walked toward the patrol van parked on the side of the street. Another man was sitting in the driver seat, waiting for his comrades. As I watched them drive away, I knew that my timely response had earned my freedom.

Soon after, I began to wear a maghnaeh. After a few trials and errors, I could keep it in place without having it slip backward. By now, the shops displayed the *manteau* in their front windows. The manteau was a long, drab-colored, Islamic version of a trench coat, and was the new fashion in modesty for women. I also began to wear a manteau to cover the curves of my body. As my hijab (my body covering), I preferred the maghnaeh with manteau instead of the all-encompassing chador. I could no longer go out in public as I had in the past.

CHAPTER 19

The Downhill

To take my mind off Ebi's dangerous working conditions near the front, I joined Mom for tea at the British embassy, hosted by the ambassador's wife for the foreign wives of Iranian nationals. For the handful of English and continental women still in Iran, the British embassy was a comfortable and familiar place of refuge. The women had formed a group and referred to themselves as the "Foreign Wives Club." Their goal was companionship and support, and to survive in Iran. The majority of this small club's members were American and English by birth; the rest were about equally split among Thai, French, Irish, Dutch, and Canadian women. Mom and one other woman had lived in Iran the longest. The younger women looked to their predecessors for advice and guidance. They would exchange recipes and English-language books, swap clothes, tell jokes, and talk about their families.

The ladies also hosted frequent get-togethers at each other's homes, and I had known many of them and their children since my childhood. Mom's friends welcomed me with open arms. They gave me the honorary title of "foreign daughter," and I referred to each of them as "Auntie." (The other *doerageh* children with whom I had been friends with since childhood were now studying abroad.)

Among my aunties in Tehran, I felt that I was back home and in my element. I was no longer a new wife and new mother in the less cosmopolitan city of Shiraz. In the embassy's large main room, I admired the hanging portraits of past and present British royals and national heroes and enjoyed sitting in the private garden. We discussed the war, the hijab, the limitations of our daily lives, and our families. The recent wedding of Prince Charles to Lady Diana Spencer was a major topic of interest. Since the Iranian media had not covered the summer 1981 event, we relied on the English-language clippings sent by relatives abroad.

According to Iranian law, the wife of an Iranian man, regardless of her birthplace, is considered to be an Iranian national. Thus, all of the club members were Iranian citizens. Mom and Sandra, an Englishwoman married to an Armenian Christian, were the only two married to religious minorities. The other married women and their children were looked on as Muslims. These foreign women had financial means and were able to travel abroad with their husbands and children. They escaped the war by taking extended European holidays and staying at their villas along the Caspian Sea. However, as wives of Iranian men, they needed their husband's written permission to travel out of the country.

In some respects, the religious minorities were treated differently. For example, travel restrictions imposed on the Jewish community limited their ability to leave the country. There were no laws that were passed on this issue, but it was unofficially close to impossible for Jews to leave Iran as a family unit. Every detail regarding the exit of a Jewish minority from the country was a complicated ordeal. Since the beginning of the war, I knew of many Jewish families who wished to emigrate. But they had encountered many problems as the special government office responsible for granting passports had refused their applications. Therefore, I too was not able to renew my passport.

Some Jewish families resorted to unconventional methods. One family converted to Islam and got their passports. A few others, whose last names ended in "ian," a common suffix of surnames among Armenian Christians, left Iran under the pretense that they were Armenian Christians. Other families were separated: usually, the wife and children left, while the husband remained behind. Many members of the Jewish families who were left behind then resorted to illegal means to flee Iran, which entailed a treacherous journey through the desert. Ebi and I would not even consider this option. We would never take part in such a dangerous and illegal scheme, especially now that we had a baby. There was no way for all three of us to get out of Iran together.

*

Mom had taught me to "make the best of every situation," and she had always been a practical person. So, after completing the short typing course in Shiraz, I decided to become a private English teacher in our home. Alongside the people calling for "Death to America," another sector of society wanted their children (and themselves) to learn English—mostly with the unspoken goal of leaving Iran.

Adhering to Islamic law, I taught only women and girls, and boys younger than eleven years old. I had small classes of four to five children each and gave private lessons to women. Teaching was a respectable job that brought in a reasonable income. Mom later borrowed my idea and began teaching English at home in Tehran to women and children.

At the end of his mandatory service a month later, Ebi joined Leora and me in Tehran. We, along with Mom and Dad, decided to spend a few days in the northern part of the country, to be as far as possible from the war. We packed some essentials and settled into Dad's Paykan for the few hours' drive from Tehran to the Mazandaran Province along the coast of the Caspian Sea.

Ebi was an excellent driver, and Dad sat beside him in the front passenger seat. Chalus Road, with its panoramic views and tunnels that cut through the mountains had always been a spectacular adventure. To our left were the jagged, reddish rocks of the cliffs, and to our right was the steep precipice to the Chalus River and the valley below. The mud houses in the canyons reminded me of the small, colorful game pieces in Monopoly.

Driving on Chalus Road required strong nerves and steady hands. The twisting, dangerous road had only two lanes, in opposite directions. All vehicles, from large trucks and passenger cars to fast motorcycles, shared the road, which was the shortest route from Tehran to the north. When passing a slow car, the driver had to proceed with caution into the opposite lane and look out for approaching vehicles. Due to the spiraling road, the driver had limited visibility of any oncoming traffic.

Our expanding view confirmed how high we had traveled. I felt uneasy when I noticed that there were no barriers along the edge of the road. A few plastic cones provided a token of protection. I wondered how many passengers had plunged to their deaths.

We passed quaint villages along the way. A man clutched the harness of a donkey balancing a heavy load of Persian cantaloupes. The children wore plastic flip-flops, T-shirts, and loose, pajama-bottom pants with elasticized waists. The women held their chadors around their faces. Some had toddlers standing by their side. I wondered what they did all day. Life could be challenging and tedious in this part of the world.

A rooster with colorful feathers was sunbathing outside a store. The shopkeeper, a bent old man, got up from his chair and greeted us. On display behind the counter were open stacked trays of eggs, an assortment of feta cheeses, and pickled vegetables. Jars of a variety of jams and many cans of tuna were neatly arranged in one corner. I wandered into a nearby stand selling colorful buckets and shovels, local artwork, and scarves and straw hats. I considered buying a straw hat to protect me from the blazing sun but decided it would look ridiculous with a headscarf beneath it. I opted for a few hand-painted wooden spatulas instead. We went back to the car, and I dozed off with the baby asleep in my arms.

I was awoken by a loud screeching sound. Our car was going downhill fast. The source of the noise was Ebi's frantic effort to pump the brakes with his foot, to no avail.

Dad was screaming at the top of his lungs, "Ebi what are you doing? Hit the brakes! For God sake, hit the brakes!"

We swerved in and out of the opposite lane, somehow missing the cars coming from both directions. For a split second, I admired how my competent husband avoided danger at every turn while trying to control our runaway car. Oh my, God! We were going to end up at the bottom of the valley, half a mile below. We were going to be today's Chalus Road statistic on the evening news.

Ebi tried to quell his own frantic fear, "I can't! I can't! I'm hitting the brake pedal to the floor, but the car won't stop. The brake is useless!"

Ebi took a sharp sway at the steering wheel to avoid the mountain, and I hit my head on the side of the door. Mom was frozen in shock. Leora woke up from the commotion and began to cry. Other drivers honked their horns and tried to avoid us. My breath remained in my chest as the car continued to twist and turn. I did not know which form of death would be easiest: a head-on collision with oncoming traffic, crashing into the jagged rocks to our immediate left, or falling off the cliff into the valley below.

Ebi kept his eyes on the road and continued to steer. He honked the horn several times to alert oncoming traffic. He did not have the option to drive the car to an open area or into bushes to slow down the car. I sensed that he was doing his best to keep the vehicle on the mountain side of the road. He paid no attention to our frantic cries and continued his firm grip on the steering wheel to maintain some control. His right foot pushed the clutch down as he shifted into a lower gear. He kept pumping the brakes to rebuild some pressure in the braking system. Suddenly, he pulled up the handle of the parking brake with his left hand. The car, which had now picked up speed as the roadway went downhill, began to spin around a few times. We were about to have a head-on collision with the wall of rocks.

The impact was loud. I checked my baby and myself for any injuries. Traffic from both sides came to a standstill, and people rushed toward us. They asked if we were okay and offered to help. They said they had been "sure we were going to fall off the cliff and into the valley."

We stepped out of the car. There were some scrapes and scratches but nothing serious. Fortunately, I did not see blood on anyone or on the seats. Dad's glasses were broken, and he was shaken up. The front of the car was crumpled, but all five of us had survived.

*

The sun was setting when we finally arrived at the seaside town of Ramsar. In my opinion, Ramsar is the most beautiful town on the Caspian coast. The last time I had been there was the summer of 1977, during a ten-day overnight camp. I still had the photograph of me standing in the water, posing in my orange polka-dot bikini. The memories seemed to have been from another lifetime, but in reality, it had only been a few years.

We checked into the hotel, which overlooked the town and sea. Mom and Dad wanted to rest. Dad was quiet and did not talk much. He needed time to process that we had cheated death and were lucky to be alive. We left the baby with them, and Ebi and I took a stroll on the beach. I listened to the waves and smelled the salt water. I bent down to collect a few seashells. Standing back up, I saw a large wooden sign: "To preserve the moral values of our society, the beaches are segregated into Brothers and Sisters areas."

Since the revolution, the two genders were addressed as "brothers" and "sisters" and had to be kept separate. The new establishment had succeeded in segregating the schools, but how was it going to separate people in a natural environment? They had divided the beach into two sections: the women to the left, and the men to the right. The boundary was marked by large wooden poles, with huge pieces of white cloth tied to them, hammered into the swimming area of the sea. The women's area was smaller, and young children and boys up to a certain age went with their mothers. I did not know whether to laugh or cry.

I turned to Ebi and sarcastically said, "Moses parted the Red Sea, and now, Khomeini has parted the Caspian Sea."

Ebi responded, "The Caspian Sea is really not a sea but the largest lake in the world."

"Who cares? It should be in the Guinness Book of World Records as the first sea to be gender segregated."

He nodded, and I continued, "Just a few years ago before we met, I was here with my friends. I would walk the sandy beaches in my swimsuit, and no one bothered to look at me. Now, a few strands of hair peeking out of my headscarf is enough to have me arrested. I can't even go in the water with my husband."

I recalled Imam Khomeini's recent statement during a speech, "Islam will put a stop to lust. Islam does not allow the women to swim naked in the sea. We will skin their hides."

I asked Ebi to wait for me while I ventured into the "Sisters-Only" area of the water. Women were legally obligated to go in the water in full hijab. During my past visits, I would lie on my beach towel and feel the sun's rays on my bare skin. Today, my navy manteau and maghnaeh made me more uncomfortable and warmer than I ought to have been.

A few local women who had ventured into the water in full clothing and headscarves, had tied their chadors firmly to their waists as they exited the water. They were not wearing bras and looked quite provocative as their wet clothes clung to their breasts when they exited the water.

That evening, far away from the urban noise of Tehran, I listened to the soothing sound of the waves lapping the shore. This was still the Caspian Sea Riviera that I had always loved.

CHAPTER 20

The Second-Class Citizen

Since the revolution, the world I once knew had turned upside down. According to the Constitution, the Twelver Imam Shia branch of Islam was the official state religion. The three non-Islamic religious groups (that is, Zoroastrianism, Judaism, and Christianity—each of which pre-dated the founding of Islam) each had a representative in the Majlis, the Iranian Parliament, and were "recognized." However, the Baha'is were deemed apostates.

In the new order, one's gender and religious affiliation affected his or her career prospects and their treatment in society as a whole. In the new order, all women were subject to the compulsory Islamic hijab, barred from entering sports stadiums, and discriminated against in matters of inheritance, divorce, and testifying in the court of Sharia law. Religious minorities were prohibited from holding senior government and military positions and serving in the judiciary. Belonging to the right branch of Islam and one's degree of religious observance also influenced one's position and success.

In a country that was overwhelmingly Muslim, religious minorities made up only a small percentage of the total population. They were not allowed to display any symbols or conduct any of their practices in public. And so, the average Iranian was isolated from non-Muslims and not educated about other faiths.

The Jewish community, which numbered about one hundred thousand before the revolution, had, by now, dwindled to about twenty-five thousand. Antisemitism sometimes blended with the government's animosity toward Israel. Television shows and print media denied the Holocaust and, at times, ridiculed it.

My status as a second-class citizen became evident to me on a pleasant December day in Shiraz. I left Leora with Ebi, who was home early from work. I wanted to try a hair salon in Falakeh Gaaz, an upscale neighborhood in northern Shiraz. I arrived at a modern two-story building and was buzzed in. The salon, on the top floor, was smaller than I had imagined. Two customers seated on folding chairs were chatting happily. A short, plump woman, who seemed to be the owner, was streaking a client's hair with blond highlights. A customer with a big bust and unruly black hair was seated to her left, waiting to have her hair blown dry. Next to her, a salon employee, a skinny girl with long black hair, was leaning over a middle-aged woman, threading her entire face (to remove unwanted facial hair). With a pair of small scissors, she trimmed the woman's eyebrows.

The thick curtains were open halfway to let in natural light. I knew that the window covering had two distinct purposes: to conceal any speck of light in the case of an Iraqi air-raid attack at nightfall and to hide the unveiled women inside during the day. I took off my manteau and maghnaeh and freed my hair and my body. I wore a short-sleeved T-shirt and jeans. All conversation in the room abruptly stopped, and everyone turned their head toward me.

I bowed my head in respect and said, "*Salam* [Hello]."

The salon owner looked at me and smiled, "Salam, *befarmayed.* [Hello, welcome.] You are new, and we are happy that you have found us. What brings you here?"

"I would like to have my hair trimmed, but only two centimeters. I like to keep my hair long."

The owner was impressed with my Tehrani accent and looked at my bare arms. The salon, gender segregated since the revolution, became a safe haven where a woman could take off her hijab.

"You are so beautiful and fair. Are you visiting our city?"

In a society where a fair complexion is equated with beauty, I took her remark as a compliment. "Thank you. Actually, I live here. I relocated to Shiraz a few years ago, when I got married. I'm originally from Tehran."

"We are honored to have a Tehrani in our midst. Let me tell you that this is a high-end salon. My clients are distinguished and influential people. Mrs. Dastgheib is one of my regular customers."

I knew that Ayatollah Dastgheib was the most prominent local religious leader. Every week, he led Shiraz's Friday prayers, called "Namaz Jomeh." His sermon was the highlight of the week, and thus, Ayatollah Dastgheib was referred to as the "Imam Jomeh of Shiraz." In the postrevolution Islamic Republic, the wives of the leaders were hidden from the public. Almost all leaders were married, but no one knew much about their spouses.

Nodding my head in acknowledgment, I said, "That's very nice."

"I know. Mrs. Dastgheib once asked me if the tools I use are clean. I told her, Khanum, I do not have any Johud [a derogatory word for a Jewish person] clients here to make my tools najes [unclean, impure]. Everything I use is clean!"

I was speechless. I knew that by referring to the Jews, she meant anyone who was non-Muslim. Until about sixty years prior, before the Pahlavi era, the dehumanizing doctrine of the ritual uncleanliness of non-Muslims had resulted in the separation of these groups from the main society. Non-Muslims were confined to live in distinct neighborhoods known as the "*mahaleh*" (ghettos). They were denied their civil rights and limited to making a living in undesirable occupations. (Dogs and pigs were also perceived as ritually najes.)

The paranoia of perceiving non-Muslims as impure forbade a Muslim from touching any item that had been handled by such inferiors. During rainy days, religious minorities were forbidden to leave their homes due to the popular belief that their impurity would wash away and spread to the general population. When grocery shopping, they were forbidden to touch the fruit and other food items. This ideology gave way to forced conversions and extended to the persecution of the followers of the Baha'i faith in mid-nineteenth-century Iran.

These discriminatory practices ended when Reza Shah Pahlavi rose to power in the mid-1920s. He was a contemporary ruler who took drastic and unorthodox measures to modernize the country. The King had considered the Shia clergy's influence in the everyday practices and attitudes of Iranians to be outdated and superstitious. Dad had once told me that Reza Shah was the first Persian monarch to pay respect to the Jews "by praying with them in a synagogue when visiting the Jewish community of Isfahan. For the Iranian Jews, Reza Shah was the second-most respected Iranian leader after Cyrus the Great."

Reza Shah's changes had many positive consequences and freed Iran's non-Muslim population to pursue higher education, advance in business and commerce, and to become productive members of society. Jews were finally free to live in any neighborhood they desired and were given equal status as citizens. Women, too, were granted more rights and privileges. Going against the Iranian clerics, Reza Shah emancipated women from the Islamic dress code of the hijab. In 1936, removing the veil became mandatory for women, and they began to dress like their Western counterparts.

Despite new liberal legislation, deep-rooted beliefs were slow to evolve and lingered in the psyche of many Iranians, especially those living on the rural outskirts of urban areas. For example, a custom that endured until my father's generation was inserting the religious identity of non-Muslims in the middle of one's name. My father had the word "*Kalimi*" (Jew) inserted between his first and last names on his civil identification documents and academic diplomas. At times, he was treated unfavorably once his religious identity became known. Dad had told me that when he was a child in Isfahan, antisemitism was simply a part of daily life.

I felt fortunate to have been born during the reign of the second Pahlavi monarch, when women were free to choose how they dressed and religious minorities were integrated into mainstream society. Most of the Jewish community lived in middle- and upper-middle-class neighborhoods of a few large cities, among neighbors who were well educated and had been exposed to people of other cultures and nationalities. But even in those years, I had wondered about many what-ifs. What if something happened to the Shah? What if, one day, his nemesis, the clergy, succeed in ruling the country? Now the what-ifs had become reality, even when I was in a beauty salon, looking for a haircut and nothing more.

I smiled sweetly at the hair salon owner and pretended that her remark was just an innocuous snippet of a casual conversation. As she trimmed my hair, she praised me for my appearance. But to myself, I vowed never to set foot in that place again, because her ignorance and dehumanizing approach had given her the moral justification to reason that others with different beliefs were inferior to her.

*

The following Friday, on December 11, 1981, the top news in the country was the martyrdom of Ayatollah Dastgheib and seven of his companions in Shiraz. A female suicide bomber had approached the cleric and his aides after they led the weekly Friday prayers and blew herself up. She was a member of the Mojahedin-e-Khalq opposition group.

Given the assassination of its most important local religious figure, Shiraz was in a somber mood. The media rebroadcast the late Ayatollah's past sermons and proclaimed a few days of mourning. Guarding the regime's strict principles also became a priority. The morality police came out in full force to inspect citizens on all aspects of civil conduct.

A few months prior, we had been spending a day with friends on the outskirts of Shiraz and were stopped for inspection. Our friend respectfully opened the trunk of the car and stood back as the bags were searched. He mentioned that, as a pediatrician, everyone relied on him to have some sort of medication with him, which the soldier soon found. The guard carefully rewrapped the children's cough syrup in its protective sleeve and put it back in the bag. After we had driven away, our friend could not stop laughing as he told us that he had filled the children's cough syrup bottle with the forbidden wine.

The morality police also checked the validity of the *mahram* relationship between the sexes, on alert for premarital relationships. They would stop couples and demand proof of marriage or a blood relationship.

During this period, Ebi and I had spent an evening with friends at a private home. Inside homes and among some of our friends, I was free to take off my hijab and sit in Western-style clothing. Before we would leave the host's home, the women would put back on their long manteau, loose pants or thick tights, and hair coverings. Some women could not be bothered with all the layers and would don a large chador, which fell over their bodies like a tent.

On the short drive home, I held our sleeping daughter in my arms. We were eager to get home because the baby had a soiled diaper, and I was concerned that she might get a rash. As we approached the intersection, we saw a checkpoint. The male morality police officers were verifying the passengers' identification.

I turned toward Ebi in frustration at being stopped and complained, "It's nine in the evening. For goodness sakes, I have a baby in my arms! Isn't this enough identification that we are married?"

"They also want to check our breaths for the smell of alcohol, and the car for any foreign VHS tapes."

I brought my head covering down over my forehead and buttoned the top button of my manteau.

The skinny teenage soldier hollered, "*Eist*! [Stop!]" He walked toward the passenger side of the vehicle, and I rolled down the window. The soldier lowered his head and leaned toward the inside of the car, "Identification cards!"

While Ebi was looking for our documentation, I carefully held the baby's smelly diaper under the soldier's nose.

The young man pulled his face away to get some air. He did not bother to wait for Ebi. He quickly motioned his right arm and ordered us to pass, "It's okay. Go!"

Ebi and I laughed all the way home. I had provided the morality police sufficient evidence of our mahram relationship.

CHAPTER 21

Public Life, Private Self

In Shiraz, like in many other Middle Eastern cities, the usual hustle and bustle began at sunrise. I looked forward to waking up at 5:30 a.m., before Ebi had to go to work and while the baby was still asleep. Our downstairs neighbor Zahra and I would go for a power walk. We passed through the doctors' villas and apartment buildings to the main streets of Khalili and Affifabad. On the way, we would pick up groceries and get excited to find rarities, such as potatoes. By noon, the commotion would end. Almost everything would quiet down after the *azan* (call to prayer) for midday invocations, when shops and businesses closed for the afternoon break, and the streets were desolate. Almost everyone relaxed for lunch, followed by an afternoon nap to rest and recharge. Then, like magic, the engines of life started up again, and everyone was ready for the late evening.

Like Ebi and I, Zahra and her husband, Dr. Kazeroni, epitomized the double lives led by a small sector of Iranian citizens. In public, we adhered to the Sharia laws of hijab and segregation of the genders. We acceded to the codes of conduct, such as appropriately praising the officials who were running the country. All this changed dramatically when we were in the privacy of our homes. At the Kazeronis' dinner parties, Dr. Kazeroni offered whiskey to their guests, and the women were dressed in the latest Western fashions. Kazeroni paid a steep price to obtain the illegal substance, and, if it was found, he could be subject to many lashes.

One day, Zahra and I planned to visit the Grand Vakil Bazaar for spices, fabric, and kitchen utensils. Just as Zahra and I got to the main street, a city bus came along and stopped in front of us. I held my toddler's hand and followed the other women who climbed the two steps to enter the bus through its middle door. We were pushed further toward the back by the next boarding passengers. Through the windows, the sun's rays beat down on us all. I held my daughter in one arm and hung onto the frayed black strap with my other hand while trying to keep my posture straight. Leora was irritable and rested her head on my chest. The clanking sound of the gold bangles of the elderly woman sitting across from me and the loud cries of the driver announcing the stops created a synchronized harmony. I noticed that the front of the bus was comparatively empty, with only a handful of men seated.

"Zahra, let's go and sit in the front. It makes no sense to stay back here."

"We cannot do that, Jacqueline joon. Where have you been, girl? The buses are now gender segregated. Men sit in the front and women in the back. We can't go to the front."

I thought of the African American Rosa Parks during the 1950s in Alabama and her determination to fight for her civil rights, refusing to cede her bus seat to a white passenger. While I admired Parks's courage, I was not going to attempt any of her tactics. To be separated by gender on public transportation was a strange experience for me. In prerevolutionary Iran, I never gave much thought to where I would sit on public transit. But now, just like all the other women, I was obligated to follow the gender-segregation rules and had to sit at the back of the bus. Otherwise, I would be arrested for breaking the law.

The schools, beaches, and hair salons had already been segregated by gender, so why was I surprised by the new seating arrangements on public transportation? I recalled my father's advice to not challenge the authorities. Just that morning, I had heard about Sadegh Ghotbzadeh, Iran's first postrevolution foreign minister, who had accompanied Ayatollah Khomeini on the Air France flight to Iran three years ago. He had been executed for allegedly plotting the assassination of the Supreme Leader and the overthrow of the Islamic Republic.

I began to make my exit by maneuvering my way along the edges of the vinyl seats, being careful not to slip on the smooth platform. Once off the

FIG 12. At age twenty-three, Shiraz, 1984.

bus, Zahra and I walked a block to the entrance of the ancient bazaar. A large banner, in Persian, was tied way up on either side of the entryway: "If a woman shows one strand of her hair, in her afterlife she will be hung from that same strand of hair for eternity."

I could not be bothered to know which cleric had authored the quote, but its message was clear. The regime had passed legislation in 1982 making the hijab mandatory for all females regardless of religious faith. Violating the hijab code was punishable by fines and imprisonment. I pulled my maghnaeh forward to make sure it covered my forehead, and we entered the bazaar.

I always enjoyed shopping at this magical place. I was a city girl, accustomed to department stores and boutiques in Tehran and in London. Here, I felt I had stepped into *The Thousand and One Nights* story of Scheherazade that our maid Mahbobeh used to tell me as a child. The bazaar's long, narrow, winding walkways formed a maze that continued as far as the eye could see. The high, arched ceilings added to the beauty of the architecture and kept the interior cool in the summer and warm in the winter.

The market was a hidden treasure to locals and tourists alike. The narrow thoroughfare had two facing rows of stalls containing a kaleidoscope of bright colors. An assortment of spices and golden turmeric was stacked in big bins and sold by the scoop. The smell of fresh herbs, dried lemons, and loose-leaf teas in large containers filled the narrow walkway. *Tasbih* (prayer beads), some made from amber, were displayed on low stools, and maroon, handwoven Persian rugs were stacked on the floor. At the request of a potential customer, the merchant would instruct his assistants, who were usually skinny teenage boys, to roll back a corner of each rug for inspection. Beautiful, colorful silk fabrics were on display from every angle of the shopkeepers' stalls. From a pile of folded children's clothing by the side of the wall, I bought a Chinese-made embroidered dress for Leora. The children behaved and held their mothers' hands in anticipation of a plastic toy as a treat. It was always fun to come to the bazaar.

*

Our across-the-hall neighbors, Forouzandeh and Dr. Farmayesh, were the opposite of our neighbors on the first floor. Forouzandeh stayed home and made elaborate dishes and took care of her son. Zahra, on the other hand, never cooked, spent her husband's money in the shopping plazas, and drove her sons to extracurricular activities. Forouzandeh and I spent hours at each other's homes, sharing recipes and keeping each other company. But Zahra was the friend who accompanied me to the northern part of the city known as "Tapeh Televisyon" (Television Hill) to purchase Persian pistachio ice cream and sit on a bench enjoying every spoonful. This neighborhood, one of the city's nicest, was where the Shiraz television station was built on a mountainside.

*

One evening after dinner, Ebi and I sat down to watch TV. We had a choice of three channels, which aired programs from about five to eleven in the evening and an additional two hours during midday. Most of the broadcasting was raw footage of the ongoing war between Iran and Iraq. All reports pointed to the fact that the Iranians had once again been victorious in these battles. The broadcast did not mention the correct number of casualties and the real horrors of the war, such as the planes that airlifted hundreds of wounded soldiers to the hospital where Ebi worked.

Furthermore, the clerics, who had become the new celebrities, now had their own programming. They still lectured and gave guidance on religious and family matters and direction as to the right path of existence. The most valuable advice was how to be frugal in times of war and save on everything we could.

That evening, we watched Ayatollah Montazeri lecture about the Jewish seventh-century tribe of Bani Qurayza. I turned up the volume. During a battle with the Muslims, all the men of the Bani Qurayza tribe were killed, and the women and children were taken captive. The Ayatollah's animosity wasn't toward Israel but toward the Jews, going back to the inception of the Islamic movement. He then declared that, upon the return of the Twelfth Hidden Imam, Mahdi, the Jews will be hunted down, even if they are hidden behind rocks and trees.

I turned off the television and said, "You know, Ebi, before I was born, my family spent a year in England so Dad could pursue a fellowship in meteorology. He wanted to advance his country rather than to contribute to the brain drain. So, they returned to Iran and built a home here. The majority of my mother's career was spent in American organizations. At one point, when I was a young child, my parents received an offer to apply for a green card to America. I could have been raised in England or America."

"Iran still has a significant Jewish and Christian community. They can say all they want in the media, but the average Iranian respects the religious minorities."

"As a doctor, your profession and education are highly respected."

"That's true, but the way things are going, I may contribute to today's brain drain."

At that moment, we were surprised by a knock on the door. From behind the door, I asked, "Who is it?" (I wanted to confirm who it was so that I would know if I had to go and get my hijab.)

A quiet whisper responded, "It's me. Zahra."

I opened the door and saw my friend with her index finger over her lips. She wasn't wearing her hijab because she had run up the stairs. "Sh! Talk quietly. I don't want Forouzandeh to hear our conversation. Is Mr. Doctor home?"

"Yes, Ebi is here."

"Very well. Both of you follow me and come downstairs. I have something to show you."

"Leora is sleeping."

"You should come down for a few minutes. Trust me. You will want to return home as soon as you see what I have to show you."

I could not understand what she was talking about. We followed Zahra to their apartment, and Dr. Kazeroni came forward to greet us. "Ebi joon, I have something to show you. It's a valuable addition to our home."

He then motioned with one hand toward the living room. Sitting below the television was a large appliance. I was too excited to stop myself, "Oh, my God! You have a VHS player? My mom has told me how some of her friends have them. But how did you get it?"

Zahra rolled back her shoulders with pride, "Eighty thousand tomans (a super unit of the official currency, the rial) will get you one."

"Wow, that is expensive."

Her husband continued, "From now on, we will be getting foreign movies. Ebi, come over and help me connect this cable as discreetly as possible to your television upstairs. This way, when we want to watch something, we will let you know, so that you can turn on your television and watch it too. Just keep it between us. We don't want anyone to know."

"But how do you get your hands on foreign movies? My mom told me that in Tehran the 'movie guy' comes over to her friends' houses once a week, hiding the movies in a briefcase. We live in an enclosed area for the doctors and their families. How can a stranger come here?"

Zahra had answers for all my questions. "Jacqueline joon, you are so naïve. We will have to go and get the movies ourselves."

"But from where?"

"Do you know that small grocery store a few blocks north on Khakshenasi Avenue?"

"Yes."

"Well, from now on, you or I will be buying our milk and cheese along with renting a movie from the young man who sits behind the counter. He will wrap it in a brown paper bag. There won't be much time to discuss the titles. Just mention you want an Amrikaee (American) or a Hendi (Indian) movie. Whatever he gives you will be better than the garbage they shove down our throats as entertainment on TV."

From that night on, our lives became a little brighter. We had no clue what we would be watching once our neighbors alerted us to turn on the television. But it was always a pleasant surprise. We watched Las Vegas variety shows, *E.T. the Extra-Terrestrial, Raiders of the Lost Ark*, and some movies that we had never heard of before. The movies were in English, and we made sure to keep the volume low. The next day, I would explain the details to Zahra, who did not understand English.

Twice a week, she would ask me to join her downstairs to watch an Indian movie together. Although we could not comprehend the spoken words, it was still possible to follow the storyline. We loved the drama, the colorful saris, and the dancing. Leora would wrap a large scarf against her small frame and twirl around, moving her head from side to side, saying a few words in Hindi.

Such small acts of defiance had emboldened the less observant to be different in private than what was expected of them in public. Private parties became a place of refuge from the restrictive reality of the outside world. Men and women without the hijab interacted and enjoyed forbidden music and drinks. To combat this problem, the Basij force carried out party raids. The arrested were fined heavily and sometimes endured physical punishment, such as flagellation. I, however, did my best to play by the rules.

*

Ebi was the only Jewish doctor that we knew of who had remained in Shiraz after the revolution. All our friends were Ebi's colleagues, who either worked at the university or were in private practice. One day, we were pleasantly surprised to be invited to the Jewish wedding of a family member of one of the radiology technicians at the hospital. The wedding was held at Homa Hotel, the most luxurious hotel in the city, which was adjacent to Azadi (Freedom) Park. It had been built less than a decade earlier, during the 2,500-year festivities at Persepolis, almost an hour's drive away. I looked forward to the opportunity to get to know some members of the small Jewish community of Shiraz.

The wedding was held in the early afternoon. We left Leora with Zahra for a few hours and drove the short distance to the hotel. Ebi and I arrived at the vast hallway of the lobby to the small banquet hall. Tall vases of fresh flowers were placed on some of the side tables. I was dressed in a long manteau that came to my mid-calf, accompanied by a large navy blue maghnaeh. When we opened the door, I gasped.

About one hundred people were present, and genders were seated together in the same room. Women were dressed in beautiful gowns; their hair was done, and their faces were made up. Everyone was joyous. The bride and groom sat on a loveseat in the corner of the hall. Complying with Shirazi Jewish tradition, a beautiful green veil covered her white dress. We joined the other guests at a long table to peel fruit and talk.

I turned around and was amazed to see wine in the center of the table. "Oh, my God! You are serving alcohol? It is one thing for men and women to mingle without any physical partition, but wine, too? You are acting as if the Islamic revolution hasn't happened in this country."

One of the guests at the table said, "This is a Jewish ceremony. The new law allows the religious minorities to abide by their customs and traditions. They know that the religious minorities make their own wine."

"But the wine is meant for religious rites."

"The religious minorities don't have restrictions on consuming alcohol. We are required to drink some wine on the Sabbath and at ceremonies. We are different."

The man sitting across from us at the narrow folding table explained how the red grapes were chosen and washed in huge tubs. He narrated the process of making the wine: First, comes the trampling upon the grapes, and then they are transferred into large barrels where they are kept in the dark basement. The older the wine, the better it got.

Ebi asked, "Aren't you concerned that this party may attract outsiders?"

"We know what to do. You just enjoy the party. We have paid the right people plenty of money to keep them happy."

Half an hour later, the party came to an abrupt stop. We heard a ruckus coming from the other side of the hall, and all conversation ceased. Women instinctively grabbed their hair coverings and held tightly to their children. The morality police had raided the wedding festivities. They arrested the groom and a few other men. Possibly, more money had to be paid for their release.

Bending the rules of the new order was a risky game. Unlike at my wedding, at this marriage ceremony, no one hollered "Mazel tov!" and "Mubarak!" The party ended on a sour note, and we got up and went home.

CHAPTER 22

Half of the World's Beauty

It was official. The news on the radio and in the newspapers announced that, after three years, the universities had reopened. All higher education was now purged of Western influences as well as un-Islamic students and professors. A friend, a medical student at Shiraz University, had called in the morning in great excitement. For her, the ordeal was over. All she had to do was to show up for class and continue her science curriculum. I, on the other hand, had an unpaved path ahead. I would take the entrance exam, and, once accepted, I would attend school in a veil and mind my own business. All I wanted was a college education.

To my disappointment, I soon realized that my acceptance into higher education would be impossible. A significant number of openings were reserved for family members of the martyrs and the wounded of the revolution and the Iran-Iraq War. They would receive preferential treatment for access to higher education. Furthermore, dedication to Islam became the single-most-important criterion for admission. No matter what one's intended field of study, each candidate also had to take entry tests in Shia theology and ethics. I finally gave up on my hope of receiving an education.

More bad news followed, concerning a colleague of Ebi's at Sa'adi Hospital. Ebi came home from work looking pale and startled.

I asked, "What's wrong?"

"They killed him."

"Who are you talking about?"

"Dr. Faghihi. A speeding motorcycle passed him as he was crossing the street in front of the hospital. He was shot at point blank. It happened this morning. I think this was done in retaliation. He had reported one of his patients, a member of an opposition group, to the authorities."

"Was the patient a member of the Mojahedin-e-Khalq opposition group?"

"Most probably. While the young man was recuperating from surgery, he was arrested and taken away."

Soon after, the hospital was renamed from Sa'adi (a famous medieval Persian poet) to Martyr Doctor Faghihi Hospital.

*

Ebi took a week off from work to process the death of his friend and colleague. We used this time to visit his family in Isfahan. By now, I understood the local vocabulary and accents of the people of Isfahan and of Shiraz, which differed greatly. I also realized that Dad and Ebi had adopted the more mainstream Tehrani accent. The bus ride from Shiraz to Isfahan took about six hours, and we made the trip a few times a year. I had begun to appreciate the famous Persian quote *"Isfahan nesf-e jahaneh"* (Isfahan is half of the world). The statement implies that if you have had the chance to see this beautiful city, you are already ahead of the game because it will seem as if you have already covered half of the beauty and wonders of the world.

Ebi's parents, Malka and Aziz, as well as three of his siblings, lived in Isfahan. Their house consisted of several rooms, including a kitchen overlooking the garden and a large living room with three tall windows. The light-filled living room was appointed with impressive handicrafts, silverwork, and rugs, all made in Isfahan, which reminded me of the same local art that we had in our home in Tehran.

White and yellow daffodils were planted in the garden, and red potted geraniums were lined up under the tall pomegranate trees. On the east side of the enclosed area, freshly laundered clothes, secured by wooden pegs, hung neatly on the clothesline. The branches of a large fig tree hung over the small pond, where goldfish swam around the small fountain located in the middle of their world. Behind the clothesline, a grapevine climbed over the back wall and stretched out over the top. The still unripe green grapes, fondly known as "*ghooreh*" in Farsi, hung from the twisted and tangled leaves. They were soon to be picked and used in a celery, herb, and meat stew.

I learned about the two temperatures for food: cold and hot. *Sardi*, or the cold category, drains one's energy. *Garmi*, or hot food, restore one's energy. There always had to be a balance during a meal or else one would become ill. The irony was that I had been brought up with Mom's English customs, which violated the food rules, and this had not caused me any problems. I also became acquainted with *sekanjabin*, a traditional beverage made with sugar, mint, white vinegar, and a dash of honey.

During the summer, the extended family gathered in the courtyard overlooking the garden and ate dinner under the star-studded sky. After dinner, the elders shared the hookah, the traditional method of smoking tobacco from a standing pipe with a glass bowl. Except for one younger brother in the United States, Ebi's other siblings were married and had children of their own. Once a week, the younger brother would call home from Texas.

Most afternoons, we picnicked along the banks of Zayandeh Rud, a large river in central Iran. We sat under the arches of the high Siosepol Bridge, also known as the "bridge of thirty-three arches," and ate *faludeh*, a frozen treat made from starch, sugar, rose water, and noodles. The children chased butterflies and ran after each other along the edge of the water. My father played here, too, as a child and told me about this city with nostalgic longing. But Dad would also remind me that growing up in this holy city had not been easy as a religious minority.

In the center of the city was the grandiose Imam Square, formerly known as the "Shah's Square." Ornate calligraphy of prayer verses embellished the entrance of a mosque. Other historic buildings that were once the palaces of Persian kings dated back many centuries. No wonder the tourists who used to visit Iran before the revolution always included Isfahan in their itinerary. I asked a store owner how tourism had changed.

He looked at us with a sad expression. "This place was once filled with foreigners, but the tourists nowadays are Iranians from across the country."

Once, when I was taking a stroll on the tree-lined boulevard of Chahar Bagh (Four Gardens), a woman dressed in a traditional, long, layered dress approached me. Her choice of clothing made me aware that she was a roaming fortune-teller looking for her next customer. She had a small frame and a pleasant smile. A few strands of her hennaed hair peeked out from her head covering. (The dye is believed to strengthen the hair.) She praised my wide eyes and the shape of my lips. I decided to go along and see what this psychic had to tell me. She took my right hand into her hands and intensely studied the lines of my palm. Lifting her head, she looked directly into my eyes, and, for a brief moment, our eyes locked. I felt a pleasant shiver down my spine from the intimacy of her gaze and her handgrip.

She began to predict my future. "You will go to a faraway land. Yes, far from here, and you will have a happy future."

I was amused by her prediction. As a Jewish minority, it was close to impossible for me to get a passport and an exit visa to leave the country. I began to pay attention to her other predictions.

"You will have two children: a girl and a boy."

For a second, I dismissed her words. What better prediction would any woman want to hear? But in a country where most people had more than two offspring, why had she stopped at two children? I gave her some money and took her predictions as mere entertainment. Although I didn't believe in psychics, I remained optimistic that what she had predicted would one day come true.

*

My in-laws lived near the Bazaar of Isfahan. That afternoon, Malka and I walked to the main shopping area. Malka wanted to buy a gold necklace for Leora. Many Iranian women from all sectors of society spend a significant portion of their money on gold—both for personal adornment and as an investment. Gold jewelry stores lined the main streets, as well as fabric stores and boutiques selling expensive items, and a variety of food markets for meats, fruits, and nuts.

As we approached a jewelry store, we heard a loud commotion and melodramatic praying in the boulevard. As I turned my head, I saw people running toward the street to join the crowds. I realized that this was another funeral procession for a war martyr, a frequent occurrence in the streets that ran toward the cemetery. Isfahan was known as a sacred city, and its inhabitants had offered the most volunteer soldiers and martyrs of the war. The casket was being carried on the outstretched arms of men in black shirts. The men chanted hateful slogans toward Iraq's president, Saddam Hussein, and America, while the black-chador-clad women followed the male mourners. The children among the two groups emulated the grown-ups.

Malka took me by the arm and said, "Let's get out of the way and go inside the store."

The following day, I got up early to accompany my mother-in-law to a friend's house. When I came out of the guest room, I was dressed in black pants, ugly black shoes, thick socks, a gray manteau, and a navy maghnaeh. "I'm ready."

Malka took a long look at me and hesitated for a few minutes. "Listen, Jacqueline joon. Don't you go to your private dinner parties at your friend's homes in Shiraz?"

"Yes, I do."

"Then make every effort to find and buy yourself a pair of red shoes. I know you can't wear colorful clothes and shoes on the street, but please don't wear drab colors indoors. Now, go and wear something nice under your manteau and put on some makeup. We will be in the car."

Malka wanted to show off her daughter-in-law to the members of her small community. Her courage and defiance of the status quo never ceased to amaze me.

Dad decided to join us in Isfahan for a few days. He also intended to go with the extended family to a pilgrimage site known as "Serah bat Asher."[1] Translated from Hebrew, the term refers to Serah, the daughter of Asher, who was one of the twelve sons of the biblical Jacob. According to legend, not only did Serah possess great beauty and wisdom, but she was also an accomplished musician. When Joseph was reunited with his brothers in Egypt, he sent them to the land of Canaan and asked them to return to their father, Jacob. But, he ordered them not to alarm their aged father, who believed that Joseph had passed away. The brothers asked Serah to sit with Jacob and reveal the fact that Joseph was still alive while she played the lyre.

The Jewish community believed that Serah had once passed through the village of Lenjan on the outskirts of Isfahan on her way to the Land of Israel. She happened to die there, and an old shrine on the grounds was named in her honor. I was pleased that the legend honored a woman.

We left Leora with one of my sisters-in-law, which gave her the opportunity to play with her cousins. Ebi and I, along with Dad and the rest of the family, arrived in Lenjan and walked through the graveyard on the site. We stopped in front of one plot with a tombstone—the grave of my grandmother Shoshana. Dad recited the Kaddish (mourner's prayer). For the first time in my life, I watched my tall, larger-than-life father quietly wipe away a few tears from his eyes. At the graveside, I met a rabbi who accompanied a bent-over old woman with a pleasant smile. She wore a loose robe and a headscarf and kissed me many times. She was my father's aunt, my grandmother Shoshana's sister, and the only surviving relative from that generation.

From the graveyard, we walked to the shrine of Serah and descended its steep stairs. We bent our heads as we entered a small crypt with a few windows. Ebi and I each lit a memorial candle to honor the deceased and placed them near each other. To everyone's amazement, as the candles melted, they twisted and leaned against each other, and faded away as one unit. I felt fortunate that, unlike my siblings Raymond and Victoria, I had visited Isfahan and experienced and learned about our paternal legacy.

CHAPTER 23

Front of the War, Front of the Plane

In Shiraz, Ebi's colleagues Homayoon, who had attended our wedding in Tehran, and Feraydoon sat in our living room waiting for Ebi's return from the hospital. They were eager for their friend to join them on their usual Friday morning hike in the Baba Koohi mountains. I served tea and tried to make small talk, but my mind was elsewhere.

Homayoon tapped his fingers on the handle of his tea glass, "Where is Ebi? Why is he taking so long?"

Casually, I said, "He had to go to the hospital and get some test results."

Surprised, Feraydoon asked, "What test results?"

Evasively, I said, "He'll be home before you know it."

At that moment, we heard Ebi's key in the door. Grinning ear to ear, my husband took one look at me and said, "It's positive."

Homayoon and Feraydoon rose with excitement. "Mubarak! This is fantastic news."

I recalled the prophecy of the fortune-teller in Isfahan, "You will have a girl and a boy." It had been four years since I arrived in Shiraz, a stay that I had expected to last for, at most, two-and-a-half years. By now, Leora was in preschool, and I had hired one of the teacher's aides to help me with afternoon chores at home.

*

I had a relatively easy pregnancy, except for the usual morning sickness during the first trimester. One particular morning, I wasn't feeling well and experienced spells of shivers and constant thirst. My face felt hot, and my lips were dry and chapped. I called the nearby Motahari medical clinic, named after the cleric Motahari, the head of the Council of the Islamic revolution who was assassinated in 1979 by an antirevolutionary group. I was given an appointment to see the doctor that same morning. I decided to take a walk through the shaded streets of the neighborhood to get to the medical building.

I got Leora dressed, and we stepped out of the house. On our way, we passed the grand murals of martyrs heroically dying in battle scenes painted on the sides of the buildings. I dropped off Leora at her preschool and continued with the walk. The layers I had on absorbed the sun's rays and retained much of the heat, but I still managed to enjoy the walk.

Once I got to the clinic, I climbed the few steps, and, after entering the building, I turned left toward the "Sisters" assigned area. This was the place where every female's conformity to the prescribed dress code was inspected. I peeked through the opening of the curtain and entered the small quarter.

A female morality police officer, covered with a black chador, was waiting for me. The first thing the inspector did was to sniff around my face and neck for any trace of perfume. She took a good look at me from top to bottom. I knew she couldn't find anything to pick on. The look on her face showed her sense of power over me. She snatched a tissue out of the tissue box and gave it to me.

"Take off your lipstick."

"I haven't applied any lipstick."

"I said take off your lipstick. Your lips are too red."

She was right. My slight fever and flu-like symptoms had caused my dry lips to become darker than their usual color. This fact made me realize that no trace of lipstick would be imprinted on the tissue. This made me feel bolder.

"I said I don't have any lipstick on. Can't you see?"

I took the tissue and with much force rubbed it over my lips.

"Here, see for yourself. There is no trace of lipstick on this tissue. My lips are naturally red!"

She gave me a sarcastic look.

"Yes, I can see you are V-E-R-Y beautiful."

I took the stairs to the third floor, where the doctor's office was located, all the while thinking that one of the worst aspects of the dress code was the harsh treatment of girls and women in public spaces by other women acting as morality police.

*

On July 29, 1984, around 3:30 a.m., I awoke with labor pains and told Ebi. A few hours later, we left Leora with our neighbor Zahra and headed to Hafez Hospital. Katayoon, who was both my friend and my doctor, was already waiting for me. Due to the shortage of some brands of medicine, I was one of the few expectant mothers in the ward to receive labor-inducing medication.

Our son was born at 11:45 in the morning. He cried from the top of his lungs and shook his hands uncontrollably. The nurse standing beside me poked my side and proudly said, "You have a son!" At twenty-three, I welcomed the blessing of becoming a mother for the second time. I was no longer the same person I was at Leora's arrival. I felt more responsible now that I had two children who relied on me for almost everything.

We named our son "Navid." The name, meaning "good news" in Persian, was befitting of the addition to our family. However, sometimes at home and for religious ceremonies, we called our son "Daniel."

*

A few weeks later, I went to Katayoon's office for a checkup. Since the revolution, female gynecologists and obstetricians were in high demand among religious women. The line to her second-floor office extended down the stairwell and into the street. I, on the other hand, as her friend, did not have to stand in line and waited only ten minutes.

Among Katayoon's patients was a Qashqai woman, one of the nomads who migrate according to the season. Every summer, they herd their flocks of goats and sheep from the highland pastures north of Shiraz to the warmer, more southern lands near the Persian Gulf. Their way of life is amid nature, and their homes are tents in the desert. Distinguished by their traditional colorful dress, every year they passed through the city and went about their business.

The Qashqai patient wore a bright tunic with side slits over pants layered with billowing skirts in red, green, and yellow. Even her headscarf, which covered the nape of her neck, was attractive and bright. The nomadic tribes of the desert were exempt from the color restrictions that we had. She was the only burst of color in the waiting room among ladies dressed in black, navy, and gray hijabs. Her husband had a thick mustache and wore wide-legged trousers.

Except in documentary films, I had never before seen a Qashqai. Standing beside her, hearing her accent, staring into her beautiful, sun-kissed face, I admired her spirit.

*

By late November, still at war with Iraq, a new routine had been imposed on us by the enemy, and my anxiety—especially as a mother of a toddler and a baby—rose. At ten o'clock each evening, radar detected Iraqi planes crossing the border. From a designated radio station, the sirens would howl. We had at least one radio set on this particular wavelength at all times. The robotic alert was always the same: "Attention! Attention! The signal that you are now hearing is a declaration of a state of red alert. This means that an air raid is imminent. Please proceed to a shelter."

The shelter usually meant remaining at home in the basement, which had the least number of windows. Many families, though, did not have a basement and would gather in the middle of their house.

An hour or two before the nightly air-raid signal, I would become apprehensive. We could only go to sleep after the ordeal was over. Instead of settling down in our bedrooms, our family of four slept on blankets spread on the floor of our small foyer by the front door to rest a bit and await the nightly siren. I would sleep in full hijab.

Then, every night, as soon as we heard the announcement of a red alert siren, Ebi and I would grab the kids and the flashlight and run to a large storage room in the basement, where the four families of our building would huddle for at least thirty minutes. Sometimes, we had other neighbors from the villas join us. The interior storage room was supposed to be safer, but

FIG. 13. Me with my husband, Ebi, and children, Leora and Daniel, at the port city of Bandar-e Bushehr (on the coast of the Persian Gulf), 1985.

I knew that we were still in grave danger. In the case of a direct hit—or even a nearby hit—we would be killed, and being in the basement would have made no difference. When each night's ordeal was over, we would go back to our apartments, pick up the blankets from the foyer floor, change our clothes, and go to sleep in our own beds.

One evening, we waited in the foyer until midnight, and nothing happened. I thought we were given the night off. A few hours later, at 3:30 a.m., the air-raid siren went off. I wrapped a blanket over Daniel, and Ebi grabbed Leora's hand. We all hurried down the staircase to the basement as fast as we could. We had been caught off guard and were half asleep due to the unusual timing of the siren.

Dr. Farmayesh, our next-door neighbor, fumbled with the keys to the storage room, but he could not open the damn door. It was dark, and our nerves were shattered. Finally, we got into another storage room. Forouzandeh turned on a flashlight for a moment, so that we would not bump into anything. I glanced around the room. Mounds of furniture were covered with sheets and had accumulated a layer of dust. In the corner, several sealed cardboard boxes were stacked up, and a few rugs were folded on top. I held Daniel in one arm, and with my other arm, I felt my way through the room by tracing the grooves of the wall.

We heard footsteps in the hall and opened the door to allow the other two families in the building to enter. Tayebeh took one corner of the rug on top of a cardboard box and said, "Jacqueline, help me spread out the rug so that we can sit on it before Forouzandeh turns off the light."

"I have a baby in my arms."

Her husband, Dr. Sadeghi, lost his temper, "Stop talking, and turn off the light! Any flicker of light can give away our hiding place. I will help you do this in the dark."

Within a few minutes, our eyes became accustomed to our dark cave. We sat in silence, each praying in his or her own way for the doomed cloud of death to please spare us and fall on some other unlucky candidate. The children fretted and became cranky as they had been disturbed from their sleep.

Ebi said, "Saddam Hussein is playing a psychological game with us. Everyone in the city was expecting a ten o'clock attack, and now he is changing the rules."

We heard a loud boom. And then, nothing. I felt as if my heart left my body, banged against the wall, and came back into my chest.

Dr. Sadeghi slapped his palms together and fixed his gaze to a corner of the room. He opened his mouth, and with a sad expression, he said, "I wonder who tonight's unfortunate victims are. Their number came up in the lottery of death."

His words sent a shiver down my spine. My legs felt paralyzed. Tomorrow's news on the radio would understate the number of martyrs from the attack.

*

A few months later, Ebi had to serve in a war zone again for one month. As was the annual ritual, I prepared for the month's stay in Tehran with Leora, age four, and Daniel, four months. I was always apprehensive about taking a domestic Iran Air flight. The commercial fleet predated the revolution, and since the revolution, obtaining spare parts had become difficult.

This was a stark contrast to my youth when my family had traveled on Pan American. By the early-1970s, my mother was working at Pan Am Airlines. She always looked elegant and stylish in her cherry red and cream uniform. Mom assisted mostly American and European travelers with reservations and claims for lost luggage. Occasionally, on my days off from school, I would accompany Mom to work. The airport was the one place in all of Tehran where my two distinct worlds intersected. Due to my fluency in Farsi and English, I would assist her in making reservations for the crew of the many airplanes that flew to Tehran to stay at the Tehran Intercontinental or other high-end hotels in the city. On a normal day, one could see up to five or six Pan Am airplanes parked on the Mehrabad Airport tarmac. During the era of the Shah, a group of advisors from Pan Am had moved to Tehran to improve the operations of Iran Air and bringing it up to international standards.

Now I was living in a country that had inferior airplanes for the safety of its own citizens. People accepted the situation by relying on a few prayers to overcome science and the lack of proper maintenance and hoped for the best.

We boarded the plane for Tehran. I held Leora's hand and carried Daniel. Fortunately, we did not have to go far. Our seats were in the first row on the right-hand side of the aircraft. I had requested extra space because I was traveling with two small children.

The plane was filling up fast, but, to my surprise, except for our two seats on the right, the front of the plane remained empty. Finally, close to departure time, six men boarded and quickly occupied the seats behind me. The flight attendant drew the curtains to offer privacy to the prominent passengers in the first-class cabin. Two men remained standing by the door when a man in a black suit stepped onto the plane. They occupied the seats across from us, in the same row.

I was sure that they—the leader and his bodyguards—were each concealing one or more weapons. I made sure that my maghnaeh fully covered all the strands of my hair. I remained still and directed my gaze toward the front or at the children. Out of the corner of my eye, I noticed that the leader smoothed his black beard as he settled into his seat and fastened his seatbelt. As the plane slowly moved on the runway in preparation for takeoff, the men began to recite their devotions aloud. The prayers became faster and louder with the roars of the engine as the plane picked up speed and started to lift off.

The aircraft gained altitude, and the leader sitting across from me turned to me and smiled at the baby in my arms. "Is it a boy?"

I made sure to keep my gaze down toward the baby. "Yes."

"What's his name?"

"His name is Navid, and he is four months old."

He took no notice of my daughter. But he could not stop looking at the baby, "Where is his father?"

"My husband is currently serving at the war front. He is a doctor and is treating the wounded soldiers."

The man was impressed. "Your family is in Tehran?"

"Yes. I will be staying with my parents while my husband is away."

Upon arrival at Mehrabad Airport, I was given preferential treatment by the bodyguards. They carried my bags and respectfully cleared the path for me to proceed.

*

It was always a pleasure to be back in Tehran, and at the house that reminded me of how good life used to be. My parents were overjoyed to see the children, but Ebi's precarious situation was always in the back of our minds.

One morning, I accompanied Dad to the local grocery store. Ever since my uncle Darius and his family left Iran for the United States during the revolution, I was Dad's closest confidante. We would take long walks and talk about our situation in Iran. I was able to supplement what my mother could not, which was the societal and cultural issues that only a native could comprehend.

As we stepped into the shop, I noticed a flyer affixed to the front window. It contained a black-and-white photograph of Fareed, one of the two brothers who had rented the third floor of my parents' house. Fareed and Kamran, sons of one of Dad's distant cousins in Isfahan, were students of the University of Tehran's medical and dental schools, respectively. Dad had a soft spot for anyone who wanted to pursue a degree in the sciences. As a favor to their father, Dad had promised to watch over them.

The lengthy obituary under the photo stated that Fareed had attained the honor of martyrdom while fighting the war with the Iraqis. A black ribbon had been taped across the image to mark his death. A week before, Fareed had come downstairs to say farewell to my parents. (His brother, Kamran, had already left Iran, during the revolution.) We stared at the picture for a moment in amusement.

To dodge the mandatory draft, Fareed had embarked on a dangerous and illegal journey through the desert terrain across the border. Dad had been worried about him because of so many horror stories about police checkpoints and the border patrol, who shot at anyone crossing over illegally. Fareed would also have been at the mercy of the smugglers guiding him through the barren wasteland. Possibly, he had to spend a night or two in the small villages along the outpost and wait for the right opportunity to cross the border either into Pakistan or Turkey. Obviously, this announcement was part of a decoy to distract any speculation about his disappearance.

The storekeeper turned to us and said, "He used to come by almost every day. He was an avid reader and asked for the daily newspaper. Did you know that he was going to be a doctor? But now, he has been elevated to the rank of a martyr. We are humbled by his sacrifice."

Dad nodded his head, "Yes, he was a righteous young man who served his country. Possibly one day, our street will be renamed in his honor."

Once back in Shiraz, Mom called and told me that Fareed's treacherous journey had ended successfully. He was ensconced in Boston, Massachusetts. Soon after, we heard that Fareed had enrolled in medical school at an American university.

CHAPTER 24

"The Martyr"

I was excited to receive an invitation to join my neighbor Forouzandeh and her friends at her apartment across the hall. Although our backgrounds were worlds apart, Forouzandeh and I had become close friends. Her invitation was a chance for me to meet new friends over tea and cake and to discuss our challenges as young mothers. The afternoon of the gathering, I got Leora and Daniel ready and knocked on their door.

Because I lived in the building, I was the only one who had arrived without a hijab. The other guests were devout and strictly adhered to traditional customs. Once inside the apartment and among themselves, the women took off their black chadors or large maghnaehs and loose manteaus. The early spring day was chilly, and we were all dressed in jeans or trousers and long-sleeved tops.

About fifteen of us sat on folding chairs and other furniture in the large main room. The children played in an adjacent room, and we could easily supervise them due to the apartment's open floor plan. The atmosphere was casual, and the conversation was friendly. In the company of these women, I decided to listen more and speak less. I wanted to know more about their lives and family issues that were different from mine. We did, however, have many shared interests, such as raising children, where to shop, and how to cook certain dishes. When the topic of polygamy and sigheh (temporary marriage) arose, tensions flared.

One lady commented, "I would prefer to witness my husband's funeral than him taking a second wife."

Another guest opposed the first woman's remark and defended the practice. "Sigheh is a great solution to many problems that women face. Like widowhood. Do you know how many women are widows? They have lost a husband to the war and the revolution. What are they supposed to do? By being in a marriage, they will be financially secure and protected. Sigheh also benefits women because it obligates the husband to provide for any children created from such a temporary arrangement."

Sipping our hot tea, we heard footsteps coming up the staircase, and then a key turning in the door. Who could this be?

Forouzandeh jumped up in surprise. "It's my husband! He is home early!"

My first thought was, "Why should this be a big deal? So what if he is home early? He will come in, say hello, and go to another area of the house: his study, the kitchen, or wherever." Evidently, the other women had a different first thought. The arrival disrupted our peaceful social gathering. The women were apparently concerned and fretted over what to do next. Some had their hijab draped over the backs of their seats. Others got up quickly to get their veil. Women nervously pulled their chadors over their heads or their maghnaeh and grabbed their manteau.

Because I had not left the building, I had not brought my hijab. I was not sure what to do. I thought about running to another room, and while the husband was talking to the ladies, I could go across the hall to my apartment and get my hijab. Another option was to borrow a scarf or maghnaeh from one of the guests who had also donned a chador on top of what she was wearing underneath. I had to act fast and blend in with the others.

I was sitting in a private home and modestly dressed—albeit my hair was not covered. So, I told myself to stay put and not to move. Dr. Farmayesh, a gentle and soft-spoken man, entered the room and approached our circle. He looked around the room to greet the women. While sitting in my chair, I looked him in the eye and acknowledged his presence. My reasoning proved to be correct. He asked me how Ebi was and sent his regards. He then acknowledged the other women and left the room. Our social gathering continued, and no one questioned my behavior.

*

The following October, my mother-in-law, Malka, stayed with us for a few days in Shiraz. Just like my parents did, Ebi's parents would periodically visit us and especially enjoyed spending time with the children. Malka was an inspiration and an invaluable resource, giving me advice on all aspects of life.

One day, Malka and I ventured out by taxi to the busy shopping area of the city. She suggested that we make a short stop at the main synagogue that was a few blocks away. Except for a few nurses and technicians at the hospital, Ebi and I did not know of any other members of the local Jewish community still in Shiraz. Our old landlords, the Soheilis, had left Iran before the war.

Malka and I opened the front door of the simple two-story building that looked like a large house from the outside. The courtyard was paved with twelve-by-twelve tiles that had been, once upon a time, white. A few trees, planted in no particular arrangement, provided an island of green. Fallen orange and yellow leaves were scattered on the ground.

The plain synagogue was in stark contrast to the city's main mosque and mausoleum, which I also had recently visited with Forouzandeh. The Shah Cheragh, built in the twelfth century, has a large dome covered in spectacular blue tiles, flanked by two spires of conventional Islamic design. Inside, glistening chandeliers hang from the high ceilings, and glass mosaics line the walls. The expansive courtyard has a square pond with fountains in the center.

Today, I was in humble surroundings. A few scooters were parked at the opposite end of the courtyard. The tall, narrow windows of the sanctuary were open onto the courtyard, adding to the illusion of space. This seemed odd because it was Thursday, and weekday services are usually less well attended than Saturday's. To Malka's and my surprise, all the courtyard chairs were occupied by male congregants, and the sanctuary seats remained empty. An additional stack of folding chairs was leaning against the wall.

As tradition dictates, men and women sit separately during services. Malka and I took the stairs to the second-floor balcony, the assigned women's gallery. It looked filled to capacity. I spotted two empty seats in the front row and sped up to reach them. The prime location would enable us to look down on the events below.

In a small community where the members know one another, our unfamiliar faces gave us away as nonnatives. We made small talk with the lady sitting next to us. I was relieved to introduce my mother-in-law and allow her to take over the conversation. I could sit back and did not have to translate any words and explain her origins.

Today, though, locals were not in a chatty mood. The atmosphere was somber. A few women wiped tears from their eyes. A hush came over the crowd, and the noise died down. All attention fell on the bimah, the raised platform in the middle of the main floor.

The leader of the service ascended the two steps to the bimah. Behind him on the wall above the ark holding the Torah scrolls hung a framed portrait of a seven-branched candelabra known as a "menorah." Obviously, there was no sign of the six-pointed Star of David, which was then associated with the Zionist regime.

A second gentleman joined the first on the bimah, and both began to recite a solemn prayer. Today was not going to be a joyous morning where the Torah would be brought out, and people would gather after the service and catch up on the latest news. Something seemed off.

I could hear the loud sound of many footsteps outside. Through the side windows, I saw that the courtyard gates were propped open. Scores of soldiers of the Pasdaran (Revolutionary Guard) entered. The uniformed soldiers, wearing tall, black, laced boots, marched in unison. Looking straight ahead, they filed into the sanctuary and took up all the chairs.

A blanket of fear spread over me as I squeezed my mother-in-law's hand. I had had two prior experiences of the outside world invading the privacy of the Jewish community. The first was when our synagogue in Tehran was used as a polling place for the referendum to vote for the Islamic Republic of Iran. The second incident was when the morality police raided a private wedding ceremony and arrested the groom and a few other men.

The chosen leader of the Revolutionary Guard in the temple was a bearded man with an unyielding stare, who I thought had probably never smiled in his life. Joining the two other men on the platform, he said, "The clear stance of the Jewish community in supporting the Islamic Republic's establishment is a testament of their obedience to the tenets of the revolution."

I wanted to ask him if we had any other choice.

He continued, "Both of our teachings are from divine faiths. We have come here today to pay our respects to our fallen fellow comrade. He is also granted the honor of being a martyr, giving his life fighting against the infidels and all evil."

Oh, my God! As I listened, I realized that this was a service for a twenty-three-year-old Jewish soldier who had lost his life at war with Iraq. Every male citizen over the age of eighteen is mandated to perform military service in Iran. Before the revolution, serving entailed little, if any, danger. Given the ongoing war, not only did military service in postrevolutionary Iran involve the possibility of death, but civilians who were regularly targeted by Iraqi fighter bombs were also in danger of losing their lives.

PART 5

Resolve

1986–1987

CHAPTER 25

Welcome to First Grade

Leora turned six in September 1986. Two days later, she started first grade at a new, all-girl elementary school. At this young age, she started wearing the hijab. My daughter's uniform consisted of navy blue pants covered by a long, shapeless, gray manteau and a large, navy maghnaeh that extended from her head to the middle of her chest. Despite her somber uniform, Leora was excited and held her new backpack tightly.

Ebi was upset when he saw Leora. "Why do they subject such young children to wearing the hijab in a building where all students and personnel are female? The walls are tall. No one can peek inside. Why the hijab?"

I felt the same way. By then, gender segregation was the norm, and same-sex schools were established through the twelfth grade. I quietly mentioned that he should watch what he said in front of the child. "Let her be happy and feel some joy in her little world." But, I was upset. Unlike Ebi, I had experienced wearing the mandatory hijab, and I did not want the same for my daughter.

In the school courtyard, Leora and I saw long lines of young girls, all dressed exactly alike. Only their facial features and hands were visible. A teacher stood in front of each line, corresponding to each grade. On the far end, the principal stood on a raised platform and spoke earnestly into a loudspeaker. I squeezed Leora's little hand and gave her a reassuring look.

FIG. 14. My daughter, Leora, age six, first grade in Shiraz, 1986

Parents, who were mostly the mothers, were invited to join their children for the first hour of school.

I stood beside Leora in line, and we followed her new classmates and their parents to the classroom. The room looked colorless and felt cheerless. It had no joy. The parents and their children sat on iron school benches. A faded and yellowed curtain covered the window. The only thing in mint condition was a framed picture above the chalkboard of the Supreme Leader. His piercing eyes and omnipotent presence could be felt at all times.

The teacher, dressed in a manteau and a black maghnaeh, stood in front of the class and said, "Welcome to first grade." Then, for the next ten minutes, a fifth-grader recited some passages from the Quran in Arabic. Although Iranians speak Persian (Farsi), the Holy Scriptures are in Arabic.

My attention shifted to my child. Leora was just like any other kid in the school, but she was also different. For the first time since her birth, I regretted my decision to give her a foreign official name, unlike Daniel, to whom we gave a Persian official name (Navid). I, too, had a foreign name and understood the dilemmas Leora would face. When I was growing up, my name was a source of admiration and represented my connection to the West. Now, this connection was a cause for condemnation. In public, I had retained my alias name, Jaleh, and used the alias name of Nilofar for Leora. But now in school, she had to use her official name. With or without a Persian name, Leora was part of a religious minority. How long would it take before her teacher and classmates started treating her differently? There had been an incident in Leora's preschool a year before. Leora had attended the preschool for a few hours during the mornings, thus giving me some time to catch up with my routine and, more importantly, allowing her to play with other children.

One of the teacher's aides had had a particular affinity toward me. She took good care of Leora, and most days when I went to pick up my daughter, Akhtar, the aide, would excitedly run toward me and give me a hug or a kiss on the cheek. I had asked her if she could come to my house for two hours every afternoon once she had finished her work at the school. She would be an invaluable help to me, and could earn some extra income. I liked her enthusiasm and was happy to have someone help me with my chores. On that particular day, Akhtar had some news to tell me.

"Mrs. Doctor! Mrs. Doctor! I don't think you should send Leora to this school anymore. This is not a place for a lovely girl like her."

"Why, Akhtar? This is one of the best preschools in the city."

"I know, but it is the people they accept here that is the problem. There is a new girl here."

I thought of the refugees from the war-torn cities of the nearby Khuzestan province. They had left behind all their belongings and had poured into the city of Shiraz. A hairdresser had once told me that some of her refugee clients had lice in their hair. I assumed that this new girl might have had lice too.

"Who is the girl?"

Akhtar pointed her finger to one side of the room.

"That one!"

I looked over and saw a girl of around four years of age, with big brown eyes and short hair. She was dressed in a clean, frilly skirt, white T-shirt, white socks, and black shoes.

"She looks fine to me."

"Mrs. Doctor, she was sharing her water cup with the other children."

"That is not the end of the world. Kids like to share things. That's how they play."

"But she is najes. She is a Johud, and her water is dirtied. She shouldn't share her cup with the Muslim kids."

A few seconds passed before I could respond. I had received, and continued to receive, so much kindness and happiness from so many of my open-minded Muslim friends who did not think this way. Although my daughter and I had unusual names, most people I knew attributed this to the fact that I had a European mother. I wasn't surprised by Akhtar's comment, but I rather felt sorry for her blind prejudice and ignorance. I looked her in the eye and said, "You can begin working in my house this afternoon. I look forward to seeing you." Akhtar gave me a kiss and happily turned around to go back to her work. One day, she would realize that she had been employed in a Jewish household. Maybe then, by getting to know my home better, she would change her mind.

My attention turned to Leora, who quietly sat beside me. I looked into her wide eyes and thought, "At least she has no idea that education used to be different." During the reign of the Shah, I wore cute dresses with white socks and shiny shoes. Our maid would comb and style my hair in braids or a ponytail, or keep the sides in place with colorful barrettes. My teachers, Iranian and foreign, wore pencil skirts, chiffon shirts, and high-heeled shoes. Their hair was styled after Queen Farah's beehive, which was fashionable at the time. When they walked between the school desks, their pleasant scent reminded me of Mom's French perfumes. They were kind and smiled. We learned morality stories with underlying principles of righteousness, love, and mutual respect. We recited beautiful poems by Persian poets from books with colorful pictures.

Since the revolution's success in 1979, Ayatollah Khomeini had urged the people of the nation to procreate and have as many children as possible. Everyone I knew was either pregnant or had a newborn. By the time Leora was ready for first grade, there were more students than the schools could handle. Therefore, many schools had two shifts, which alternated weekly. Leora attended school one week from eight in the morning to noon, and the next week, from noon to four in the afternoon. One day, she told us that the teacher had drawn some bottles on the chalkboard and asked the girls if anyone had them in their houses. Apparently, the state officials, through the teachers, were using children to investigate which parents had any banned alcoholic beverages.

Leora had a habit of using the front of her maghnaeh as a handy, makeshift tissue to wipe her nose; therefore, the front panel of her head and chest covering was always dirty. The back of her neck became sore from the heat rash that had developed under her maghnaeh.

An important part of her education was safety. The children had to make trenches in the schoolyard so that they could hide in them when the Iraqi warplanes appeared from above. I never understood how much security a hole in the ground would provide. The thought of not being with my child during an air raid was too difficult to even imagine.

Leora began to kiss the posters of the ayatollahs that were displayed everywhere we went. She had learned to wave her fists in the air and chant "Death to America" and "Death to Israel." She had no idea where these places were, but Leora knew that she and her classmates had to wish for their destruction. During recess, Leora and her friends would play a game where they formed a funeral procession and carried an object over their heads, pretending it was a martyr being taken to the cemetery.

Soon after school started, the two-day Jewish New Year holiday of Rosh Hashanah was upon us. I decided that I was not going to send Leora to school for the first day of the holiday. That evening, during a phone conversation with Mom, I said that I was going to send her to school the second day of Rosh Hashanah.

My mother's advice was priceless. "Jacqueline, don't you dare send her to school tomorrow. The holiday is two days, and you will keep her home for two days."

"But, Mom, we are not going anywhere. Let her go to school, although what she is learning is more propaganda than an education."

"Don't you understand? They know she is a religious minority. If you send her to school, they may think that you are Baha'i and are pretending to be Jewish!"

Mom was right. Being Christian or Jewish was easier than being a Baha'i. Two weeks into the school year, I made an appointment to meet with the principal. She was a short woman with a prominent face and round spectacles that pinched the middle of her nose. I explained our status as religious minorities and requested that my daughter be excused from the mandated religious studies. Leora would instead fulfill this requirement by attending a religious Jewish program at a private weekend school for an hour-and-a-half on Friday mornings. The principal's reception was cold. She did not even bother to raise her head as she signed the release form. I then vowed to continue to supplement Leora's education at home. Every night, I would read her stories in English and teach her different subjects.

*

It had become very difficult for Ebi and me to witness our child's indoctrination into a belief system that contradicted our own. My despair grew each day when I realized how hard it was for us to leave Iran. My passport had expired, and because of my Jewish religious minority status, it was close to impossible for me to renew it or to apply for a new one. Ebi, on the other hand, had a valid passport. He could travel out of the country, but it was almost impossible for us to travel as a family. Iranian Muslims could obtain a passport in a short time.

Ebi remained optimistic and promised me that he would find a way for us to leave Iran. I had heard of forged passports and illegal border crossings, but I knew that my husband would not even think of committing any illegal acts for fear of the harsh consequences. Only a few years before, a prominent member of the Jewish community and his wife who were given passports were detained at the airport, suspected of spying for Israel.

One day, Ebi told me that he knew the new minister of health of the province of Fars. He was a devout man and had completed his surgical training under Ebi's direction and supervision. He was the Islamic Republic's top health official for a vast region. Getting in touch with him would not have been easy for the average citizen, let alone setting up an appointment to see him. Due to the minister's respect for his former teacher, Ebi managed to have a private meeting with him.

Ebi explained that Dr. Michael DeBakey, a renowned surgeon, scientist, and medical educator in Houston, Texas, had invited him to take a course relevant to his medical practice. Dr. DeBakey had helped develop the mobile army surgical hospital, a fully functioning hospital that could be used in combat zones.[1] The doctor was an acquaintance of Ebi's younger brother, who was now living in the United States. Ebi's participation in the course would enhance his skills as a surgeon in general and in treating the war wounded in particular.

Ebi asked the minister if he would kindly write a letter to the passport officials, requesting that his wife and children be added to his passport as companions. The excuse was that this had to be done soon because the course was about to start. The minister gladly wrote the letter, which Ebi took right away to the passport office.

To my astonishment, within a few days my name, as well as the names of our two children, were added as companions to Ebi's passport. But the possession of a passport was not sufficient documentation to exit the country. We were now required to apply for an exit permit stamp. This essential component in the passport, which authorized the holder to leave the country, was more important than the document itself.

Ebi surrendered his passport to the authorities. A background check to rule out criminal activity, unpaid taxes, and any remaining mandatory military service was necessary. After the background check, the exit permit could be approved.

The law also required that, as a married woman, I needed to have my husband's written consent to travel outside the country. We needed to leave the country as soon as possible lest anything or anyone hinder our plans. In my youth, I had traveled freely without thinking much about it. One would simply get a ticket and board a plane. That was all there was to it. Now, leaving Iran was finally becoming a real possibility, and was a way out of restrictions, prejudice, fundamentalism, and war. Most important, it gave a glimpse of opportunity and a better life—maybe even my long-awaited college degree—somewhere else.

I had a few days to condense what we needed into two suitcases. We would leave everything else behind. It was a painstaking process to choose among the most precious items. I could not take too many photographs because that would seem odd for someone who was leaving the country temporarily. I gently removed an eight-piece embroidered artwork from its frames, which I had once spent hours to create, and folded it in one of the suitcases. Packing was not that difficult. Taking jewelry and gold out of the country was illegal, and I was happy to leave behind my drab clothes.

Instead of worrying about what clothing items to take with me, I decided to pack new clothes for the trip—clothes that I actually wanted to wear. I grabbed my hijab and headed out to the shopping plazas on Ghasrodasht Avenue. Fabric shops lined the street. Foreign clothes were hard to find or too expensive to buy; therefore, the preferred method, especially for women, was to buy fabric and have clothes made by a seamstress.

I entered a small fabric shop at the far corner of a shopping passage. A few women covered in black chadors were contemplating which material would be suitable for a pious woman to wear. I stood by the door and eyeballed the shelves on the wall behind the merchant for what I was looking for.

Pointing my index finger to the top row, I addressed the shopkeeper. "Excuse me. May I please see the pastel yellow denim fabric?"

He stepped on the metal stool, and with the help of a long, pointed metal rod, brought down my selection and unrolled it across the counter. I admired the cheerful color. It reminded me of the pretty yellow dresses of my childhood, and the yellow georgette dress I wore to my sister's wedding. Yellow was also the color of Dad's roses in the garden, and of gold and the sun. Yellow had been missing from my wardrobe for a long time.

I lifted my head, "Yes, please give me two meters of this fabric."

One of the women standing next to me asked, "Why are you buying this fabric? Is it for your toddler?"

Without bothering to look into her eyes, I said, "Actually, it is for me. I want to have a pair of yellow pants made for myself!"

Her grimace unleashed a chorus of sneers among the other customers.

"This is such a disgusting color for clothing."

"I can't believe your choice!"

"Thank God you won't be able to wear it in the street!"

I ignored them and paid for my fabric. I headed straight to the seamstress a few blocks away. I asked her to please rush as the pants had to be ready by the end of the day tomorrow. I was going to wear my new pants with a flowing, sleeveless blouse, once I got the chance to start a new life in the land of freedom.

Leaving my clothes behind was easy, but the harsh reality of leaving behind eight years of accumulated belongings of married life was another matter. I became occupied with small details. I found it difficult to say goodbye to our houseplants! The plants that I had cared for attentively for so long would all dry up and die. Then, I turned my attention to other possessions: my English china dinner set, my wedding photographs (all photographs for that matter), my jewelry, my favorite painting of majestic trees with fallen yellow and orange autumn leaves, and our living room and dining room furniture.

I had deliberated over every purchase and had fussed over choosing the right color for the drapes in the living room. Did I want cream? Or light green? Did my silverware complement the china? Did I chip the edge of a saucer? I had arranged the Persian rugs on our living room tiles with such care and exactitude. We were elated the day we purchased our twenty-four-inch color television. The large freezer hummed in the corner of the kitchen as if pleading not to be left behind. It was filled with washed and chopped herbs and the meat that I had spent hours cleaning and preparing. Now, all of that seemed so trivial. Never, until this moment, had I realized that the quality of one's life far surpasses the quantity of one's possessions.

For the past few evenings, under cover of night, I had heaved garbage bags full of stuff into the large curbside dumpsters. I did not want to attract the prying eyes of the bored housewives, who would have observed my suspicious activity behind their closed drapes and wondered why I had so much trash.

I had many caring and close friends in my adopted city. How long would it take for them to realize that we had disappeared? What would Mr. Haidari think when he delivered yet more sacks of produce to our house the following week? He was a gentle and kind villager whose young daughter had been operated on by Ebi a few years before. Since the surgery, without our asking, he would deliver sacks of hard-to-find potatoes, onions, and other vegetables to our home every week in gratitude. Would he be told that we have gone? Would he understand why we left? I could envision him resting his head at the side of the front door and crying as he was told the news of our quick departure. We would also become the envy of our fellow Jews left behind. I could hear their remarks in my head: "How did all of them manage to get out as an intact family?"

The evening before our departure, we hosted a few guests, the family of a prominent member of the regime. Despite an upheaval of emotions inside, I had to entertain and show a pleasant face. Ebi had performed a double mastectomy on the wife and mother of the family, who had breast cancer, thereby saving her life. Her husband, her parents, and their three children had asked to come over and pay their respects. I served hot tea and *bamieh* (a Persian sweet) in our spacious living room.

They gave us a large box wrapped in colorful paper. I opened the gift with gratitude and excitement and thanked our guests for the expensive French Moulinex household appliances, which were considered a luxury at that time. One by one, I took out a food processor, a blender, a bread maker, and a coffee grinder. Thanking them again, I knew that I would never use any of these items.

*

The next morning, I held Leora's and Daniel's hands, and Ebi carried the two suitcases. He closed the door and turned the key. Unlike when my sister left eight years before, it was no longer possible to have personal property shipped abroad and thus I was leaving everything behind for good. It was time for me to say goodbye to my beloved home, our home, and everything that was inside.

I had spent eight memorable years of my life in this city. These years had made me a better, stronger person and a more mature adult. I said a silent farewell to my friends and neighbors. Goodbye, my lovely home. Thank you for all the good times we had amid the difficult encounters. Goodbye, my beloved Shiraz.

CHAPTER 26

Why Is This Night Different?

We arrived in the afternoon at my parents' home in Tehran to say our farewells. We were joined by my in-laws and Ebi's older sister, Haleh, and her husband and their children. Both sets of parents spoke about how they had envisioned enjoying their retirement years surrounded by their children and grandchildren. They said, "Who thought the community would disintegrate, and everyone we knew would just pick up and leave?"

Leora, six, and Daniel, two, were oblivious to what lay ahead. They were happy to be at their grandparents' house and to receive so much love and candy. They ran around the spacious halls, playing hide-and-go-seek with their cousins. We all watched the kids as they ran and laughed as they discovered each other's hiding places. I kept thinking that this time, my kids are getting out, and the other kids are staying behind.

The afternoon had been emotionally draining. Ebi's mother hugged her grandchildren as tightly as she could. We shed lots of tears as we said goodbye. We forced fake half smiles for the camera as we took our last group photographs. We promised each other that somehow, somewhere, someday, we would reunite. Ebi's relatives left, and we closed the front door behind them.

I turned to Mom and told her that the sole of my right foot kept on itching. This had never happened to me before. She responded that this was a sign that I was going to set foot in a new land—one that I had never been to before. Mom had a reasonable explanation for everything. She told me to look ahead to the children's future. After her arrival in Iran, it had taken her seven years before she had returned to England. She reassured me that we might be united sooner than that. Mom sounded strong and determined, yet I could sense the heartache in her tone. If only I had had an Iranian mother, I would have known that she would be able to manage better. I felt guilty for leaving her behind.

That evening, we went to bed quite late. Who could sleep? We had an important day ahead of us. Our flight would leave Tehran at 11:00 a.m., but we had to be at the airport hours before for the lengthy and burdensome inspection process and to check in.

My parents' spacious house, my childhood home, had four comfortable bedrooms. If these had been normal days, we would have had the option of any of the guest rooms that were now vacant. In the days of the Shah, our live-in maid occupied the bedroom facing the street. But tonight, Ebi, the children, and I retreated to the dining room, which was closer to the interior, center point of the house. The dining table had been pushed aside toward the east wall to make room for the few blankets, which we had spread over the Persian rug. Mom and Dad slept in a smaller bedroom away from the main windows.

As was customary in every Iranian household during the war, all windows were crisscrossed with duct tape to prevent glass from shattering in the event of a bombing. We had heard many stories of how the glass fragments could dance through the air, acting like shrapnel, and penetrate every muscle of the body. The floor-to-ceiling windows overlooking the backyard had been taped. The ivory lace drapes of the past had been replaced with thick curtains. As I plumped up the pillows of our makeshift beds on the dining room floor, my mind was flooded with memories.

Ten years before, in 1977, during our Passover Seder, the house was filled with people and laughter and joy. We sat at the table and ate our festive meal from gold-rimmed Lenox china plates.

At the time, I was a carefree teenager, and my sister, cousins, and friends giggled as we passed the parsley and the unleavened bread, called "matzah" in Hebrew, around the table. The parsley symbolizes the coming of spring and suggests the perpetual renewal of life, while the matzah is a reminder of the Israelites' hasty departure.

Tonight, I thought about the Four Questions, which pose how and why the first night of Passover is different from other nights.

"Why on other nights do we not dip our food even once, but tonight, we dip twice?"

"Why on other nights do we eat leavened bread, but tonight, we eat matzah?"

"Why on other nights do we eat all vegetables, but tonight, we also eat bitter herbs?"

"Why on other nights do we eat sitting or reclining, but tonight, we all recline?"

Dad would clear his throat and answer, "Our ancestors had been slaves in Egypt and were deprived of freedom. We eat matzah because of the Israelites' hasty departure. They had no time to wait for the bread to rise. Tonight, we eat bitter herbs because it reminds us of the bitterness of slavery in Egypt. We dip the parsley in the vinegar or salt water to remember the tears our ancestors cried. Most important, we commemorate our freedom by reclining on cushions like royalty."

Those were the nights when we celebrated the holiday as part of our beloved community. The lights were bright, our clothes were colorful, and our hearts were filled with joy. My cousin Kami said that we lived in the best place on Earth. After the last sentence of the service, "Next year in Jerusalem," he said, "We are not going anywhere."

But why was *this* particular night so different from all the other nights? Tonight, the answer was different. Tonight was quiet, empty, and fateful. Although we did not have the symbolic foods and celebrate with family and friends, the answer was also the same: Tonight was about my hasty departure.

On the shelves of the étagère in the dining room, family photographs were neatly arranged in rows on a few of the shelves. A smiling Granny Miriam looked down at me. I interpreted her smile as wishing me well on my journey and blessing me from the other world. Had it been ten years already since she passed? At least she died knowing only that her beloved Stella was happily married and living in comfort.

In another photograph, taken when Raymond and Christine honeymooned in Tehran, Mom and Dad, my two siblings with their respective spouses, and our extended family and friends gathered in front of the water-fall at Darband. The neighborhood was on the northern edge of the city and the entry point of a popular hiking trail.

That day, we hiked the narrow trails and stepped on rocks to cross the fresh stream. Our happy faces are a testament to how good life was. There I was, holding my Revo sunglasses on the tip of my nose and making a funny face. I had felt so stylish in my bell-bottom jeans and the lavender T-shirt that I had purchased at the Bullring Market in Birmingham, just a few months before. I smiled at the memories. Except for my parents and me, everyone else pictured had left Iran.

The gaping hole in the center of the shelf was where a prized photograph had been. The photograph of Dad with the Shah, no longer on display, was once the most valuable possession in the house. For every guest to our home, Mom would colorfully recount the day when his Royal Highness personally visited her beloved Rahmat's classroom at the university. She would describe every detail of the Shah's visit as if she had been there her-self. Now, we could not have any trace of such a picture in our home. A few years ago, Mom removed the cherished keepsake from its frame and tore it to pieces.

CHAPTER 27

The View from the Rooftop

My family had moved to the Yousefabad neighborhood when I was five years old, more than two decades before. This house had been the center of my universe, and these hours were my last there. I had condensed all of our remaining possessions into the two suitcases by the front door. I stared at the black maghnaeh and the gray manteau draped on top of the luggage. I was glad to leave behind all the dull coverings I had been forced to call "clothing." So, this was how everything was going to end? This was the turning point of my family's life? If everything went as planned, we would leave Iran the following morning for an unknown future in America. We had no guarantee of making it, no home, no jobs, and Ebi would need additional credentials in order to practice medicine.

In our improvised bedroom in my parents' dining room, Leora and Daniel's innocent faces peeked out from under the patterned blanket. By the time Ebi and I rested our heads on the pillows, it was already 1:30 a.m. Apprehension and other strong emotions kept me awake, and I stared at the ceiling. The radio, on low, was at the edge of my pillow.

At 2:30 a.m., as my eyelids grew heavy and my aching body settled, I jumped up startled. I had heard a fighter jet's engine in the sky, lit up by a full moon. I got up and went toward the windows, knowing well that that was not a sensible thing to do. I looked up, and there it was. I saw the pilot pass above our backyard. He was so close that I could see the earflaps of his hat. Under my breath, I muttered the Persian curse: "*Shir-e madaret haramat bashe*," which means, "May the breast milk you received from your mother as an infant become poison in your body." In other words, the pilot had grown up to be a good-for-nothing human being.

The radio station had not yet broadcast the piercing red alert siren, a prelude to some horrifying, imminent reality. The last thing we needed tonight was an air strike. I turned off the radio and shook Ebi's tired body. He hated to be woken up during the night. As a surgeon, he was routinely interrupted during his rest, and he cherished a night's sleep.

"What is it? Let me sleep. What is wrong with you?"

"We are under a red alert. An Iraqi bomber jet is above us!"

Ebi sat up and shook his head in disbelief. There was nothing more to say. I knew what he was thinking. We had made it so far, and now, this?

Out of despair, I began to pray. "Oh, God, don't mess everything up! We only have eight-and-a-half hours before we leave the country. Please, God, let us make it out."

Considering that we had traveled 580 miles inland from Shiraz, I thought we were somewhat out of harm's way in Tehran. But in Mom and Dad's house, there was no customary place to take shelter—no basement, and unlike our apartment in Shiraz, no storage room. I thought of taking the kids to sit in the parked car in the garage, the lowest point in the house, but then remembered the car had a full tank of gas. The staircase was also out of the question because it was by the glass entrance door and the large windows between the first and the second floors. I heard my parents in the adjacent living room.

"Jacqueline darling, are you awake?"

"Yes, Mom, we are here."

"And the children?"

"They are fast asleep. I turned the radio off before the siren would start. Let the children sleep. It's better for them to sleep and be oblivious to what's happening around them."

Dad interjected, "Yes. Let them sleep. We can't go anywhere. We have to sit and wait."

The house was in complete darkness. The four of us sat in the living room and would be able to hear the children if they woke up. Each of us prayed silently for this to pass and for the lottery of doom to befall someone else. It was an agonizing fifteen minutes.

Suddenly, there it was. We heard the awful sound of a bomb drop. The house shook from the intensity of the blast, and the glass windows vibrated violently. We were startled and felt sheer panic. Then, we stared at each other in stunned relief. It was over for now. It had not been us. We had been spared.

Mom turned to Dad, "The bomb must have landed in the neighborhood."

"You're right. I have never experienced it this close."

I nodded. "I can't believe that the kids slept through it. They are exhausted. However much I try to shelter them, all these experiences will inevitably cause trauma."

Ebi jumped up, "Let's go up to the roof and see what is going on."

I had always admired Mom's strength, but this time, she spoke softly, "I'm fed up with all this. I was under bombings as a child. You can't leave the kids alone. I will stay here with them."

Dad, Ebi, and I rushed to the third floor, and Dad unlocked the apartment door. (Our former tenants, the brothers Kamran and Fareed, were long gone.) We went through the short hallway onto the expansive rooftop. The third floor had half the living space of the first and second floors, as the remaining half was the rooftop.

We froze in shock, unable to process the view from the roof. It looked like a scene from *The Towering Inferno*, the 1974 movie about a disastrous fire in a San Francisco high-rise building and the efforts to rescue those trapped inside. Dad and I had seen the movie at the local theater when it first came out. I could never have imagined that more than a decade later, we would witness a reenactment of a similar drama in our very own neighborhood.

The bombing took place across the street from Shahram Hospital, near the intersection of Asad Abadi and Valiasr (formerly, "Pahlavi") Streets. The flower shop where I would meet Sima was at a nearby corner, and the Kourosh department store was one block south.

From the roof, we could see the tall condominium building that had taken a direct hit. The night sky had turned bright yellow, deep orange, and blood red, as the flames engulfed the structure from all sides. The fire danced viciously from one side to the other, leaping out of every opening of the building. I brought my hands in front of my mouth and watched in horror.

For many years, every day on my way to school, I had passed this building. At least a few hundred people lived there. Families with young children. Families just like mine. No one could have survived the conflagration. I felt blessed that my distance from the unfortunate target prevented me from hearing the victims' agonizing cries for help.

I knew that the next morning, the local radio announcer, in a matter-of-fact tone, would mention that a few hundred brothers and sisters had been martyred the evening before. It would be a sentence or two and take possibly a minute to read. I had heard this dreaded sentence on the news too many times before. Death had become a footnote to life in Iran, whether in the battlefields or in the cities.

We only had a few more hours in Iran. We had to pay a hefty price, as we were leaving our families and friends, possessions, and home behind. But that we were leaving so much behind seemed trivial after witnessing the reality of death.

*

A few hours later, we sat quietly in Dad's white Paykan as he navigated the maze of Tehran traffic to Mehrabad Airport. Mom had refused to come. She had taken a similar ride, thirty-six years before, when she left her family in England to come to Tehran, and she was not going to repeat the drive, this time to see me leave. Mom preferred to say her goodbyes at home. She promised me that she would keep a low profile and continue to teach English privately at home. I knew that Dad would take care of her, but I was deeply distraught to leave her in the wartime Islamic Republic.

Ebi sat up front with Dad, and I sat in the back with the children. From my window, I watched the streets of Tehran pass by. This was the last time I would see the murals of bearded war martyrs and read the slogans "Sister, guard your hijab" and "Death to America" written on the walls. We entered the circle where the Shahyad Monument stood. I gazed up at the massive structure. In 1971, during its construction, we watched with pride as the sloping white marble edifice rose up as a symbol of modern Iran.

Fortunately, the monument was renamed for one of the principles of the revolution, Azadi (freedom) Tower, and not in honor of a cleric or a martyr.

Dad parked the car in front of the international terminal. We got out of the car, and Dad kissed the children and gave Ebi and me one last hug. He whispered in my ear, "May God bless you! Go in safety, and just leave. Your mother and I will be waiting for your phone call from the other side of the border."

CHAPTER 28

Flight

We pushed the rickety baggage trolley through the main hall of the airport. Large paintings of religious clerics in turbans were mounted on the walls. It was crowded and loud and felt disorganized. We joined the line for inspections behind a mullah in a long robe, accompanied by two women in chadors and six kids. I tried to figure out the women's relationships to the man. Were they his wife and sister? His wife and mother? I came to the logical conclusion that they were his wives. Leora befriended one of the children, a girl who was closest in age to her. They began to play with a plastic doll that the girl held in her arms. The mullah and Ebi smiled at each other as we watched the children play. The two little girls came from two different realms, but in their simple world, all they wanted was to play together.

We were directed to the inspection screening area. Ebi and I parted ways. He took one suitcase and the stroller to the men's division, and I held the other suitcase and both children. For women, the pat down and luggage inspection were conducted behind thick, heavy drapes. Obviously, the privacy was for modesty reasons, but the curtains did nothing to block the sound of the disturbing pleas of the travelers who had entered before me. Prized possessions, such as gold pieces, loose gemstones, jewelry, and who knows what else, were mercilessly confiscated from the bewildered passengers. Such incidents could prevent a traveler from leaving Iran.

I was next in line. Ebi's mother had tried her best to persuade him that she was an expert in sewing gold coins into the linings of blazers and coats. She even hinted that she had the skill to hide paper money inside the buttons. Ebi would not allow her to carry out her scheme. "No material possessions are worth the risk. Nothing is to hinder our exit, Mom."

I stood there confidently, knowing there was nothing for them to pick on. I was merely going for a short stay, as was evident from my compact luggage (partly filled with diapers). I was modestly dressed in loose pants, a long-sleeved, knee-length manteau, and a large maghnaeh. I wore no makeup.

The screener, in a black maghnaeh and black chador, glanced at Leora and Daniel, who were obediently standing beside me. She then went through my luggage with great speed and proceeded to remove many clothing items and some toiletries. I knew my luggage was not going to give her any satisfaction of finding anything special.

I politely mentioned that we were going on a short trip and emphasized that Iran was my country. She did not bother to lift her head. She then asked for my handbag, which I quickly handed over. From my wallet, she pulled out a thin piece of paper the size of a playing card. It had intricate patterns and some printed lines in Hebrew, a language that was other than Arabic or Farsi.

She demanded, "What is this?"

"It's a traveler's prayer, to ask for a safe and uneventful journey."

Apparently, the prayer gave away my inferior religious identity. She took an amused look at the unfamiliar piece of paper. My heart was pounding. It had been in my wallet for a long time, and, out of habit, I had kept it there. Why had I not thought of removing it from my wallet before we left for the airport? What shall I do? What I wanted to do was to tell her to back off. It was not easy to think straight. The kids were becoming agitated, the space was cramped and stuffy, and the stench of her armpits was making me nauseous.

I put on a pleasant half smile and continued, "Imam Khomeini has referred to the Prophet Moses as 'kalimollah', the messenger who spoke directly to God. He was the spiritual leader who confronted the pharaoh with a cane. Our imam has also done the same, but he didn't need a cane to confront the pharaoh of our times."

I was proud to have made up such a remark at the spur of the moment, but she was not impressed. The screener looked at me with cold eyes and proceeded to crumple up the prayer in her hand and throw it on top of the luggage. With a quick hand gesture, she waved us out and told us to leave. Wasn't she supposed to give me a pat down? We exited through a second curtain to the boarding area.

Ebi, who was waiting for us, came forward to help with the children. We placed our luggage on the carousel and proceeded to the last checkpoint, Passport Control, to retrieve our passport before boarding.

Ebi looked the officer straight in the eye and said, "My passport, please?"

The officer checked over his list. I watched him raise his eyebrows as he searched the names on the paper in front of him.

"Just a moment. There is a problem."

He lifted his arm and waved to another man in uniform who seemed to be his senior officer. A large man with a thick beard came over. Both men stared at the list in confusion.

"You have just one passport for the whole family?"

Ebi responded calmly, "Yes. The minister of health of the province of Fars requested that my family members be added to my passport on an expedited basis for a program I need to attend. There was no time for my wife and children to apply for passports."

"Your passport is not here!"

"But it should be here."

"Silence!"

The officers shuffled through the papers before them. I bit my lips, and my face was ashen.

I heard an announcement that our plane was about to board: "Iran Air Flight 712 to London will be boarding shortly."

The senior officer picked up the telephone and spoke to someone in the security and intelligence department. The people who were standing behind us in line were getting restless. Pointing to Ebi, the man said, "You. Step out of the line. Hurry and don't take other people's time. Follow the guard in the uniform to the room for further questioning!"

I stood there helpless and in utter disbelief, as my husband was taken away.

Over the loudspeaker, I heard, "Iran Air passengers for Flight 712 to London, please line up at the gate."

Leora pulled on my sleeve, "Mommy, why did Daddy leave us? The lady said we can go. I want to go on the big airplane."

"We have to wait for a little while. Daddy will be back soon."

Daniel was tired of the heat and the crowds. He was beginning to rub his eyes, and I knew he was getting hungry.

The announcement continued, "Iran Air Flight 712 to London will be leaving shortly."

"Ebi, where are you? Please, God, please. Let us get out! We have come so far. I don't want the plane to leave without us. So, this is how it will end? We will make it to this point and then return home? This can't be happening."

"Last call for passengers on Iran Air Flight 712 to London. Please board the plane."

By now, the kids could not keep still. Leora was tugging at my hand. Daniel, in my arms, was crying. I pulled my headscarf further down onto my forehead, in case Daniel tried to pull it back in frustration. All we could do was wait. How much longer would this take? What the hell was Ebi doing in that room? What questions were they asking him? My eyes were fixed on the door of the room. Every second seemed like an eternity. I guess it was time to give up. There was no point. The plane that was supposed to take us to a better life was leaving us behind. We were not allowed to leave.

"Last call . . ."

Just then, the door flung open and Ebi, looking pale, rushed in. I looked at his hand. Oh, my God, he had the passport in his hand! He ran toward me and grabbed Daniel from my arms. Ebi, with his son in his arms, jostled his way through the crowd.

"Hurry!"

Hurry is what I did. Holding on to Leora's hand, I ran as fast as I could.

Ebi kept on shouting, "Wait. Wait. Hold the door. We're coming!"

We jumped onto the plane, and without waiting for us to be seated, the flight attendant slammed the heavy door behind us. We made our way through the narrow corridor of the plane to our seats.

The flight attendant stood in the front of the cabin and said, "In the name of God, the merciful and the compassionate, welcome on board Iran Air. Please fasten your seat belts."

The plane picked up speed and finally lifted off to take us to a new land

and a new life. Ebi and I stared at each other in disbelief. I looked out of the window, and for the last time, I took a glimpse at the city below. I was flooded with memories and emotions and lost in thought. This was my home, my city Tehran, my country Iran. I will miss its sounds and streets and the shady tree-lined paths of Saei Park and Shafaq Park. I will miss the melody of the water in the joobs that run down the main streets. I will miss the night sky filled with shining stars. I will miss the warm, sesame-covered barbari bread fresh out of the brick wall oven. I will miss the country where I had listened and danced to music, fallen in love, and borne my two children.

I tried to find my childhood home, my high school, and the park where I had spent so many hours of each day giggling with my friends. How do Mom and Dad feel at this moment? Will I ever see them again? I glanced at the majestic Mount Damavand with its snowcapped peaks. Mom had once told me that this mountain was her first view from the plane's window when she arrived in Iran thirty-six years before. Now, the same view will be the last scene to be embedded in my mind.

Gradually, the outline and shape of the buildings blurred together. I held onto my children. They had no idea that this journey would change the direction of their future. I felt a deep sense of appreciation and admiration for my husband, my very own Moses, who has redeemed me and would deliver me to the promised land of my dreams. My feet were no longer grounded on any land, having left one country behind and not yet stepped on another. I was in limbo, in no-man's-land.

It was time to ask Ebi the pressing question on my mind. "What happened in that room?"

"I was questioned by a nasty official, flanked by two guards. The official realized the unusual situation. We were a Jewish family of four, leaving the country with one passport. More alarming, the document had a one-time-only exit permit stamp, as opposed to the multiple exit permit."

"Then what happened?"

"I told him about my position at the university hospital, and the times I had spent in the war zone. Finally, he threw my passport on the floor and told me to *"Gom sho* [Get lost]."

Soon after, the pilot announced that we had cleared Iranian airspace. I sighed in relief. For a moment, I thought of taking off my hijab, but I was a passenger on Iran Air and would have to wait until I stepped off the plane.

A few hours later, the plane approached Heathrow Airport. London would be a stopover, and America was our final destination. America was the land that had always seemed so far away. I thought about my encounter with the fortune-teller in the street of Isfahan. Her prophecy had come true.

*

Houston, Texas, United States of America

Two weeks later I am sitting on a plush leather sofa at the home of Ebi's younger brother. It is also my twenty-sixth birthday. My brother-in-law is hosting a large crowd to celebrate the achievements of the local baseball team, the Houston Astros, in the National League West. The cheerful guests, drinking beer or wine, made chitchat about the day's events.

An attractive girl in a miniskirt sat facing me with crossed legs. She seemed disappointed and was complaining to her friends that the lady at the tanning salon had not done an adequate job. She pointed to a visible streak on the side of her leg.

The guy seated to my right recommended that we all go see the upcoming science-fiction action movie *Predator*. "It's about a team of commandos on a mission in the jungle, and they find themselves hunted by an extraterrestrial warrior." Leaning toward me, he adds, "Trust me. This movie will keep you on the edge of your seat." Turning to the group, he said, "We all need more excitement in our lives!"

I politely excused myself and retreated to the patio. In the still night, I looked up at the dark evening sky over Houston and savored the peacefulness of the moment. I had finally arrived in the faraway land of America that Mom had told me about when I was six years old. How disappointed I had been to learn that I was named after an American queen who wore plain little hats instead of a crown or a tiara. But, now, in America, with my hair uncovered and loose, a queen without a crown sounded just fine to me. I had taken the long route to get to this point, but I had finally arrived.

Epilogue

Ebi and I and our children arrived in the United States on March 18, 1987. We lived in Houston with Ebi's brother for fourteen months. I took care of the house and worked as a teacher's aide at a local preschool. Ebi's brother owned a flower shop, and Ebi waited on customers. After the flower shop closed each day, Ebi would study for the comprehensive exams to qualify to apply for a surgery residency program. (Ebi's foreign credentials were not recognized in the United States.) Eventually, he was accepted into a five-year program in the Midwest and repeated the rigorous training. One year of the program was forgiven due to his outstanding qualifications and prior experience.

Nine years after my education had been derailed in Iran, and having been in America for one year, I enrolled in college. I earned a business degree and worked as a CPA (Certified Public Accountant). Leora is a successful attorney and founded her own law firm. She has a daughter, Juliana. Daniel followed in his father's footsteps and is a surgeon. Both Leora and Daniel have few recollections of their childhood in Iran. Our family is proud that we have contributed to America and never received any assistance from the government.

By 2001, after travel restrictions for the Jewish minority had eased, my parents, widowed father-in-law, and three of Ebi's siblings as well as the majority of their families had resettled in America. In 1999, thirteen Jewish men, one of whom was sixteen years old, were arrested on trumped-up charges of spying for Israel. They were put on trial in a revolutionary court in the southern city of Shiraz and could've possibly had to face the death penalty. Fortunately, under international scrutiny, the last member of the prisoners was released in 2003. My siblings, Raymond and Victoria, and their respective families, also moved to the United States. Victoria had a second child in America. I also reunited with several classmates and my camp friend Sima.

Ten years after my departure, I came in possession of my mother-in-law's gold coin, which was brought out illegally, after it had been buried in the backyard of her house for all those years.

My parents fell in love with America and savored every minute together in this remarkable country. The highlight of their later years was when Ebi and I visited them in Los Angeles. We would sit around the kitchen table and reminisce. They shared stories of their respective childhoods in two distinct parts of the world. We discussed our lives in Iran and their recent adventures at the senior center. My father's passing in the summer of 2014 inspired me to write this book to honor his memory. Mom, now widowed, is in a culture where she speaks the native tongue.

Most Iranian Jews who left before or during the 1979 revolution moved to Southern California or the East Coast, whereas we settled in the Midwest. Southern California is home to the largest concentration of Iranians in the world outside of Iran. They represent all faiths and sectors of Iranian society. The older generation of Iranian Americans speak nostalgically about their homeland, but for the second generation, born and raised in the United States, Iran is a distant place in the East. For me, the Iranian revolution divided my life into three epochs: the period of the Shah, the time of the Ayatollah Khomeini, and my life in America, the third culture that I have come to embrace.

March 18, 2017, was a milestone for me. Thirty years after my emigration, I had lived in the United States longer than I lived in Iran. Yet, I continue to keep abreast of the country I left behind. Ebi and I watch Iranian television by satellite and follow Iranian news and politics in the local and Farsi-language press. At home, Ebi and I speak in Farsi. We speak English with our children.

Tehran and, to a lesser extent, Shiraz are now large metropolitan cities with modern amenities. Recently, a friend visited and photographed the Yousefabad neighborhood on my behalf. Given the expansion of the capital city, my old neighborhood is no longer within the northern boundaries of Tehran. Otherwise, from the photographs, I saw that not much had changed. The corner bakery and the local grocery store have been replaced by a row of newly constructed shops, but my beloved three-story childhood home remains and has not yet been torn down to make way for another high-rise. Its white marble facade is discolored with age, but the garage door is still painted dark green; the vast windows of my old bedroom loom above. My parents eventually sold the house, and I do not know who the current owners are.

Mohammad Reza Shah Pahlavi, the last king of Iran, passed away in Egypt in the summer of 1980, at age sixty. Seventeen months after we left, August 20, 1988, the Iran-Iraq War ended. The eight-year conflict took a devastating toll of death and destruction. Ayatollah Khomeini passed away in the summer of 1989, at age eighty-six. Dr. Ali Afkhami, our friend and a father of four, who had brought me a tray of dates when I was laboring at home with Leora, was executed in Iran in 1992. He was convicted of fraudulent charges of espionage and homosexuality.

In forty years, Iran's population has more than doubled—from around 35 million in 1979 to over 82 million in 2019. And yet, Iran's Jewish population is an estimated one-tenth of its prerevolution size. The current Supreme Leader, Ayatollah Khamenei, succeeded Ayatollah Khomeini and will retain his position for life. Ayatollah Khamenei has been a political fixture for the past thirty years. This means that the majority of the population has no recollection of Imperial Iran. I belong to an exclusive generation that fully experienced Iran in its three eras of the monarchy, the revolution, and the Islamic Republic.

Iran remains a country of contradictions between conservative values and modernity. With the advent of social media, smartphones, and other technologies, the youth of Iran are connected to the global community and demand more freedom and opportunities. The mandatory hijab for women and girls has relaxed to include lighter colors and a head covering that, for some, veils most but not all of the hair, and the use of cosmetics.

My impetus for finally leaving Iran was seeing our daughter Leora, age six, in hijab to enter first grade. Now, Leora's daughter, our grandchild, is six. On a beautiful sunny day in Chicago, on her first day of school, I helped Juliana pick out a navy-and-white dress with a pink floral border at the hem and pink sneakers to wear. I then adjusted the faux flower in her hair. I held her hand as we walked to school. The schoolyard was filled with boys and girls, smiling and laughing. Leora and I kissed Juliana goodbye, and she ran to catch up with her friends. I smiled as I watched her joyfully enter the building.

Glossary of Persian, Arabic, and Hebrew Terms

In Persian and in Hebrew, all words are spelled with a lowercase first letter. Terms in Hebrew are denoted by (H), and in Arabic are denoted by (A).

aba (A). Robe worn by Muslim clergy.

Abadan. A city in the South of Iran.

Allahu-akbar (A). God is great.

Amrikaee. American.

Arvand Rud. A river in the southwestern part of Iran.

Ashkenazi (H). Referring to Jews of European descent or their traditions.

Ayatollah (A). High-ranking Shia cleric.

ayd-e-shoma-mubarak. Happy holidays.

azadi. Freedom, liberty.

azan (A). The Muslim call to prayer.

Baba. Father, Dad.

"Baba ab dad, Baba naan dad." Dad gave me water, Dad gave me bread.

"Baba khun dad, Baba juon dad." Dad gave his blood, Dad gave his life.

Babolsar. A city on the southern coast of the Caspian Sea.

Baha'i. A religion that emphasizes the spiritual unity of all humankind.

Baha'ullah (A). Glory of God, the founder of the Baha'i faith.

bamieh. Persian sweet soaked in a syrup.

bar mitzvah, bat mitzvah (H). Jewish coming-of-age ceremony for boys and girls, respectively.

barbari. Persian thick flatbread.

Basij. Literally, "mobilization." A large paramilitary organization that operates under the Islamic Revolutionary Guard.

befarmayed. Welcome.

Behesht-e Zahrah. A large, well-known cemetery located in the southern part of Tehran.

beshkan. A traditional Iranian finger snap using clasped hands.

bimah (H). Elevated platform in a synagogue from which the service is conducted.

chador. A full-body, head-to-toe covering for women.

chai. Tea.

choresh fesenjan. A Persian stew made with chicken, walnut, and pomegranate paste and seeds.

chosh amadid. Welcome.

chuppah (H). Jewish wedding canopy.

Cyrus the Great. Ancient Persian king and founder of the Achaemenid Empire (ca. 600–529 BCE).

daeem. Permanent.

doerageh. A person whose parents are from two distinct nationalities.

Dokhtar Shayesteh. Iranian equivalent of the Miss America pageant.

eist. Stop.

enqelab-e farhangi. Cultural revolution

Enqelab-e Islami. Islamic Revolution.

Enqelab-e Sefid. White Revolution; the Shah's modernization programs.

estekan. A miniature glass used for drinking tea.

Esther. Jewish Queen of Persia (ca. 492–460 BCE).

Ettela'at. News. Also, the name of an evening newspaper.

faludeh. A frozen treat made from sugar, starch, rose water, and noodles.

farang. The West, referring to Europe and America.

farangi. Foreigner, usually one from Europe or the United States.

Farsi. The language spoken in Iran. Also known as Persian.

Ferdowsi. Hakim Abu'l Qasim Ferdowsi Tusi (b. Tus, ca. 935–1020 CE), a revered Persian poet and author of the epic of *Shahnameh* (The Persian Book of Kings).

Gavaznha. The Deer (title of a movie).

gaz. A white, pistachio-filled nougat from Isfahan.

ghabel nadareh. It's nothing much.

gharbzadeh. Someone who is mesmerized with the West.

ghooreh. Unripe green grapes.

Golestan Palace. One of the oldest historic palaces in Tehran.

Gom sho. Get lost.

Hafez. Khajeh Shamseddin Mohammad Hafiz-e Shirazi (b. Shiraz, ca. 1310–1380 CE) is a revered Persian poet and author of *Divan-e-Hafez*.

haft seen. A table setting of seven symbolic items beginning with the letter *s* during the Nowruz celebration.

Haggadah (H). The book used during the Jewish holiday of Passover that retells the story of the Exodus from Egypt.

halal (A). Ritually fit for consumption by Muslims.

havoo. The relationship between two women who are married to the same man.

Hendi. Indian.

hichi. Nothing.

hijab (A). Islamic covering for women.

hora (H). Israeli dance.

Imam (A). A descendant of and successor to the Prophet Muhammad. Also the prayer leader of a mosque.

Imam Hussein (A). The third revered Imam in Shia Islam (626–680 CE).

Imam Mahdi (A) (in Persian, Imam Zaman). The twelfth revered Imam in Shia Islam, who is the hidden Imam and is expected to return (b. 869 CE).

"Isfahan nesf-e jahaneh." Isfahan is half of the world.

Jahrom. A city located in the Fars province.

Jashn-e Honar. Prerevolution summer art festival in the city of Shiraz.

"javeed Shah." Long live the King.

Johud. Derogatory term to refer to a Jewish person.

joob. Water channels that facilitate the transportation of water.

joon. My dear.

Jomhuri-e Islami. Islamic Republic.

Kaddish (H). Jewish mourner's prayer.

Kalimi. A Jewish person.

ketubah (H). Jewish marriage contract.

"Khahar, hijabat ra re'ayat kon." Sister, guard your hijab.

Khamenei. Ayatollah Sayyid Ali Hosseini Khamenei (b. Mashhad, 1939–), the current Supreme Leader of Iran.

khaneh takani. Thoroughly cleaning the home in preparation for Nowruz.

khanum. Miss or Mrs.

khatam. Persian handicraft of inlaid wood.

Khoda. God.

Khomeini. Ayatollah Sayyid Ruhollah Musavi Khomeini (b. Khomeyn, 1902–1989), the founder of the Islamic Republic of Iran and its first Supreme Leader.

Khuninshahr. City of blood.

kippah (H). Skullcap.

konkoor. National university entrance exam.

kugel (H). A traditional Ashkenazi Jewish baked-noodle dish.

lavash. A kind of flatbread.

maghnaeh (A). Head-to-shoulder upper-body covering for women.

mah. Moon.

mahaleh. Ghetto, the part of a city where religious minorities were confined to live.

mahram (A). The male relative of a woman who is permitted to see her without hijab.

Majlis. The Iranian parliament. Also an assembly.

maman. Mom.

manteau. Long Islamic overcoat to cover a woman's body.

"Marg bar Amrika." Death to America.

"Marg bar bi-hijab." Death to the women who are without the hijab.

"Marg bar Esraeel." Death to Israel.

"Marg bar Shah." Death to the Shah.

Mashallah (A). "What God wanted has happened." This phrase is used to praise someone and to mention that something good has happened.

matalak. Harassing phrases men direct to women in the street.

matzah (H). Unleavened bread consumed during the Jewish Passover holiday.

Mazel tov (H). Congratulations.

MEK (A). Mojahedin-e-Khalq Organization. The largest Iranian opposition group, committed to overthrowing the Islamic Republic.

menorah (H). A Jewish, seven-branched candelabra.

mezuzah (H). A Jewish prayer scroll placed inside a cylindrical container and hung on the doorpost.

Mizrachi (H). Referring to Jews of Middle Eastern descent or their traditions.

mofsed-e fel-arz (A). A term used for the accused on trial. "One who sows corruption on Earth."

Mohammad Mosaddegh. Prime Minister of Iran from 1951–1953 (b. Tehran, 1882–1967).

Mohammad Reza Shah Pahlavi. The last king of Iran (b. Tehran 1919–1980), who was the Shah of Iran from 1941 until his overthrow by the Iranian Revolution of 1979.

mosafereh. She is a traveler

mostazafin (A). Downtrodden, the oppressed class of a society.

Mubarak (A). Congratulations.

mullah (A). Islamic cleric and theologian.

nadarad. Does not have.

nanvayee. Bread shop.

najes (A). Anything or any living being that is considered impure and unclean.

naqdeh. Delicate handmade and exquisitely ornate fabric usually embroidered with gold thread.

Nimeh Sha'ban. The fifteenth day of the month of Sha'ban, in the Islamic calendar.

noghl. A white, Persian sweet made of sugarcoated slivers of almond.

Nowruz. New Year in the Persian calendar.

ostad. Professor.

Pahlavi. Last name of Iran's royal family.

Pasargadae. The site of the tomb of King Cyrus the Great.

pasdar. A title for members of the Revolutionary Guard.

Pasdaran. The Revolutionary Guard.

Paykan. Arrow, also the name of an Iranian-made car.

Persepolis, Persian city (Greek), and Takht-e-Jamshid (Farsi). The ceremonial capital of the Persian Achaemenid Empire (ca. 550–330 BCE).

poolaki. A traditional sweet made of sugar, water, white vinegar, and saffron.

Qashqai. Nomads who migrate according to the season.

Queen Farah. Farah Pahlavi (b. Tehran, 1938–) was the third wife of the last monarch of Iran.

Queen Fawzia. Fawzia Fuad (b. Alexandria, Egypt, 1921–2013) was the first wife of the last monarch of Iran.

Queen Soraya. Soraya Esfandiary-Bakhtiari (b. Isfahan, 1932–2001) was the second wife of the last monarch of Iran.

rahbar. Leader.

rahnamai. Showing the way, leading, directing.

Ramsar. A city on the southern coast of the Caspian Sea.

Rastakhiz Party. The Resurgence (or resurrection) Party.

Reza Pahlavi. The last crown prince of Iran and the son of Mohammad Reza Shah and Queen Farah (b. Tehran, 1960–).

Reza Shah Pahlavi. The first king of the Pahlavi dynasty and the father of Mohammad Reza Shah (b. Alasht, 1878–1944). He was the Shah of Iran from 1925 to 1941.

rial. Iranian currency.

Rosh Hashanah (H). Jewish New Year.

Sa'adi Shirazi. Abu-Muhammad Muslih al-Din bin Abdallah Shirazi (b. Shiraz, ca. 1210–1292 CE) is a revered thirteenth-century Persian poet and author of the *Bostan*.

sabt-e ahvaal (A). Registrar's office.

sabzi khordan. Persian side dish of fresh herbs.

sabzi polo. Persian dill, coriander, fenugreek, and parsley rice dish.

Salam (A). Peace, hello.

sanad-e ezdevaj. Marriage license.

sang. Stone.

sangak. A type of Persian bread.

SAVAK. The national security and intelligence organization during the Pahlavi regime.

sayyid (A). Honorific title used to address the descendants of the Prophet Muhammad.

Scheherazade. The narrator in *The Thousand and One Nights*.

Sephardi (H). Referring to Spanish or Portuguese Jews or their traditions, which were also adopted by Jews from the Middle East.

sekanjabin. A traditional beverage made with sugar, mint, white vinegar, and a dash of honey.

Shab-e Yalda. Persian festival of the longest night of the year.

Shah. King.

Shahanshah. Emperor; King of Kings.

Shahbanou. The Shah's wife; title of Queen Farah (b. Tehran, 1938–).

Shahnameh. The epic manuscript about the Persian kings.

Shahyad Tower. Known as a symbol of the city of Tehran. This structure was renamed to Azadi Tower in postrevolutionary Iran.

shaytan-e bozorg. The Great Satan, referring to the United States.

shaytan-e kochak. The Little Satan, referring to Israel.

Sherkat-e Melli-ye Naft-e Iran. The National Iranian Oil Company.

sheva brachot (H). Seven marriage blessings.

sineh. Woman's breast.

sinie. Tray.

sigheh. Temporary marriage.

Siosepol. The bridge of thirty-three arches in Isfahan.

sizdah bedar. The holiday celebrated outdoors commemorating the thirteenth day of the Persian new year, Nowruz.

ta'arof. Persian etiquette of exchanging polite words and gestures.

taaghoot (A). Idols and idol worshipers.

tahdig. The crispy, golden crust of rice left to scorch on the bottom of the saucepan.

tallit (H). Prayer shawl.

"Tanha rahe saadat, shahadat ast." The only way to salvation is martyrdom.

tanoor. Oven.

Tapeh Televisyon. Television Hill.

tasbih (A). Prayer beads.

toman. Iranian currency. Ten rials are equal to one toman.

Velayat-e faqih (A). Islamic jurisprudence.

Yom Kippur (H). Jewish Day of Atonement.

Yousefabad. Author's childhood neighborhood in Tehran.

Zan-e Rooz (Today's Woman). A women's magazine.

Zayandeh Rud. The largest river in central Iran.

Zoroastrianism. Pre-Islamic religion of Persia, which is still practiced by a small minority.

Notes

HISTORICAL NOTE
   1. Ganji, "An Open Letter."

4. CRACKS ALONG THE AVENUE
   1. Woolley and Peters, "Tehran, Iran, Toasts of the President and the Shah at a State Dinner, December 31, 1977."

7. WHEN JACQUELINE MET EBI
   1. Amir-Hussein Radjy, "Rewriting the Iranian Revolution," *New Republic*, July 6, 2017.

11. UTOPIA?
   1. "The Speeches of Ayatollah Khomeini." BBC World Service.

18. "SISTER, GUARD YOUR HIJAB"
   1. Habilian Association, "Tragedy of 7 Tir."

22. HALF OF THE WORLD'S BEAUTY
   1. Kadari, "Serah, Daughter of Asher: Midrash and Aggadah."

25. WELCOME TO FIRST GRADE
   1. Lawrence K. Altman, "Michael DeBakey, Rebuilder of Hearts, Dies at 99," *New York Times*, July 13, 2008.

Bibliography

BBC World Service. "The Speeches of Ayatollah Khomeini, Extracts from The Story of the Revolution." BBC Persian Service, http://www.bbc.com/persian /revolution/khomeini.shtml.

Ganji, Saeed. "An Open Letter." National Union for Democracy in Iran, December 7, 2015. https://nufdi.net/index.php/component/k2/item/196-an-open-letter.

Habilian Association. "Tragedy of 7 Tir." Nejat Society Non-Governmental Organizations, June 27, 2012. http://www.nejatngo.org/en/posts/4571.

Kadari, Tamar. "Serah, Daughter of Asher: Midrash and Aggadah." In *Jewish Women: A Comprehensive Historical Encyclopedia*. Jewish Women's Archive, March 1, 2009, accessed January 27, 2017. https://jwa.org/encyclopedia/article /serah-daughter-of-asher-midrash-and-aggadah.

Woolley, John, and Gerhard Peters. "Tehran, Iran, Toasts of the President and the Shah at a State Dinner, December 31, 1977." The American Presidency Project (Jimmy Carter). https://www.presidency.ucsb.edu/documents/tehran-iran -toasts-the-president-and-the-shah-state-dinner.

Reading Group Discussion Guide

1. In chapter 3, Jacqueline refers to prerevolution Iran as "an idyllic, golden age of peace and prosperity." In the same chapter, her cousin Kami describes Iran as the "best place on Earth." In what ways did Mohammad Reza Shah's agenda of social reforms, secularism, and modernization shield the Lavis and other local Jewish families from religious discrimination?

2. Despite the country's growing economic prosperity during the Shah's reign, many Iranians—especially the religiously observant—perceived the dominant culture as disrespectful of their traditional Islamic values. In chapter 4, Jacqueline recalls "dining at fine restaurants on North Pahlavi Avenue and feeling the glares of waiters, doormen, and taxi drivers." Why did some citizens not feel represented by the monarchy? How did they express their discontent? Under what circumstances would you work for someone whose values conflicted with your own?

3. In the early days of the revolution, university students were at the forefront of the protest movement that demanded the Shah to leave Iran. In chapter 4, Jacqueline, in the cafeteria, "heard students, in hushed tones, express anti-Shah sentiments." What groups now felt marginalized? And why?

4. In chapter 12, Jacqueline quotes her father's advice when she learned of SAVAK, the Shah's secret police: "Never get involved with the authorities in this region of the world." Later, Jacqueline's father tells her that they must vote on the referendum because "A blank identification card is not a good thing. It may imply that your ideology is not aligned with the new regime." How is life in a nondemocratic country different than life in a free society where citizens have full voting rights?

5. Alerted by a town crier, many people claimed to have seen the Imam's image in the moon. In chapter 9, Jacqueline writes, "How gullible people had become to believe anything they were told." How were religion and superstition at the forefront of daily life?

6. In chapter 11, Jacqueline expresses her concern for the safety of her English mother during the revolution. Jacqueline writes, "Mostly, she did not leave the neighborhood unless accompanied by my dad or me. It was safest for Mom to stay at home. Even though being English, French, or Canadian was preferred to being American or Israeli, expats were still treated with antipathy as pampered outsiders." How did the rising antagonism of the masses toward Westerners in Iran affect the lives of the Lavi family more so than the average Iranian family? What made Jacqueline's mother particularly vulnerable?

7. Jacqueline would have preferred to leave the country at the beginning of the revolution, as most of her relatives and friends had done. But, in her senior year of high school, Jacqueline meets and becomes engaged to a medical doctor in Shiraz, committing her to at least two-and-a-half more years in Iran. Unlike Jacqueline, her father believed that "This too shall pass" (chapter 6), and her mother said that they couldn't just pick up and leave because of some upheaval (chapter 5). Why were Jacqueline's parents' reactions so different from her own?

8. In chapter 12, Jacqueline cringes at the stains on the Persian carpets left by the "muddy boots" of the soldiers overseeing the election. In chapter 24, during a visit to the synagogue, Jacqueline writes, "I had had two prior experiences of the outside world invading the privacy of the Jewish community." What symbolism did the synagogue have for Jacqueline as a religious minority in Iran? Why did Jacqueline feel like an outsider in her own country?

9. In the early days of the Islamic Republic, how did the new regime differentiate between Jewish Iranians and Israeli Zionists (chapter 13)? Why was one group tolerated and the other despised? What precautions did the Lavis and Jacqueline's in-laws take to show their loyalty to the Islamic Republic?

10. Like Israel, America, too, was derided. Jacqueline was then teaching English privately, and in chapter 19, she states, "Alongside the people calling for 'Death to America,' another sector of society wanted their children (and themselves) to learn English." What other contradictions are part of her experience?

11. On March 7, 1979, the Ayatollah Khomeini imposed the hijab on women in the workplace. In chapter 12, Jacqueline tells her aunt about her concern that she too, would be forced to wear the hijab. Not long after the success of the revolution, all Iranian women over the age of six were subjected to hijab. In chapter 19, Jacqueline recalls that as a teen she walked on the beach in a swimsuit and was ignored, but "Now, a few strands of hair peeking out of my headscarf is enough

to have me arrested." How did the new ideology and laws regarding women's dress restrict Jacqueline's life?

12. Toward the end of the Shah's reign, Jacqueline describes street protestors dressed in white "to symbolize a death shroud" (chapter 7). During the Iran-Iraq War, the new regime espoused reverence for martyrs, and renamed streets and painted murals in their memory. In chapter 17, Jacqueline says, "These young soldiers were told that they would go straight to heaven through the path of martyrdom." How does this theology of martyrdom—one's willingness to die for a cause they believe in—resonate with today's extremism?

13. In chapter 20, Jacqueline describes how religion and gender influences one's "career prospects and their treatment in society." How does marginalizing a sector of society through erroneous beliefs, such as the concept of being *najes* (impure), change a society? What is a contemporary example of a demographic facing discrimination? How does that alter your own perception of that group?

14. Jacqueline and her family relied on the television and radio as their primary lifeline to current events and politics, and yet, Jacqueline points out how the media manipulated the truth. After the bombing in her childhood neighborhood, in chapter 27, Jacqueline expects the morning radio announcer to matter-of-factly report that a few hundred brothers and sisters had been martyred the evening before and also to understate the number of casualties. How important is the role of the media in shaping the values of a society?

15. Jacqueline suggests that Passover, which commemorates the Israelites' exodus from Egypt to freedom, is a metaphor for her own plight. In chapter 26, she juxtaposes the customary Four Questions asked at the Seder with her situation. In chapter 28, Jacqueline refers to the Prophet Moses as she speaks to the inspecting officer. She also refers to her husband, Ebi, as her "very own Moses." How does the Passover narrative relate to Jacqueline's personal journey?

16. Jacqueline illuminates the lives of three children across time: herself (chapter 2); her daughter, Leora (chapter 25); and her granddaughter, Juliana (Epilogue). Each generation started school in a different political era and under unique circumstances. What does each child at this tender age symbolize about the social conditions and values of the particular era?